Principles
in Practice

The Principles in Practice imprint offers teachers concrete illustrations of effective classroom practices based in NCTE research briefs and policy statements. Each book discusses the research on a specific topic, links the research to an NCTE brief or policy statement, and then demonstrates how those principles come alive in practice: by showcasing actual classroom practices that demonstrate the policies in action; by talking about research in practical, teacher-friendly language; and by offering teachers possibilities for rethinking their own practices in light of the ideas presented in the books. Books within the imprint are grouped in strands, each strand focused on a significant topic of interest.

Adolescent Literacy Strand

Adolescent Literacy at Risk? The Impact of Standards (2009) Rebecca Bowers Sipe

Adolescents and Digital Literacies: Learning Alongside Our Students (2010) Sara Kajder

Adolescent Literacy and the Teaching of Reading: Lessons for Teachers of Literature (2010) Deborah Appleman

Writing in Today's Classrooms Strand

Writing in the Dialogical Classroom: Students and Teachers Responding to the Texts of Their Lives (2011) Bob Fecho

Becoming Writers in the Elementary Classroom: Visions and Decisions (2011) Katie Van Sluys

Writing Instruction in the Culturally Relevant Classroom (2011) Maisha T. Winn and Latrise P. Johnson

Literacy Assessment Strand

Our Better Judgment: Teacher Leadership for Writing Assessment (2012) Chris W. Gallagher and Eric D. Turley

Beyond Standardized Truth: Improving Teaching and Learning through Inquiry-Based Reading Assessment (2012) Scott Filkins

Reading Assessment: Artful Teachers, Successful Students (2013) Diane Stephens, editor

Literacies of the Disciplines Strand

Entering the Conversations: Practicing Literacy in the Disciplines (2014) Patricia Lambert Stock, Trace Schillinger, and Andrew Stock

Real-World Literacies: Disciplinary Teaching in the High School Classroom (2014) Heather Lattimer

Doing and Making Authentic Literacies (2014) Linda Denstaedt, Laura Jane Roop, and Stephen Best

Digital Reading
What's Essential in Grades 3–8

William L. Bass II
Parkway School District, Chesterfield, Missouri

Franki Sibberson
Indian Run Elementary School, Dublin, Ohio

National Council of Teachers of English
1111 W. Kenyon Road, Urbana, Illinois 61801-1096

Staff Editor: Bonny Graham
Series Editor: Cathy Fleischer
Interior Design: Victoria Pohlmann
Cover Design: Pat Mayer
Cover Image: Donté Jones
Text Images: William L. Bass II, Donté Jones, Ana Sibberson, Franki Sibberson

NCTE Stock Number: 11574; eStock Number: 11581
ISBN 978-0-8141-1157-4; eISBN 978-0-8141-1158-1

It is the policy of NCTE in its journals and other publications to provide a forum for the open discussion of ideas concerning the content and the teaching of English and the language arts. Publicity accorded to any particular point of view does not imply endorsement by the Executive Committee, the Board of Directors, or the membership at large, except in announcements of policy, where such endorsement is clearly specified.

Every effort has been made to provide current URLs and email addresses, but because of the rapidly changing nature of the Web, some sites and addresses may no longer be accessible.

Library of Congress Cataloging-in-Publication Data

Bass, William L., 1973–
    Digital reading : what's essential in grades 3-8 / William L. Bass II, St. Louis Missouri, Franki Sibberson, Dublin, Ohio
        pages cm
    Includes bibliographical references and index
    ISBN 978-0-8141-1157-4 ((pbk))
  1. Reading (Elementary) 2. Reading (Middle school) 3. Reading—Technological innovations. 4. Reading—Computer-assisted instruction. I. Title.
    LB1573.B366 2015
    372.41—dc23
                                                      2015003215

Contents

Acknowledgments

This book has been a learning process for both of us, and we appreciate the opportunity to think more deeply about digital reading. We could not possibly individually thank all of those who have supported us in this process as so many people, near and far, have influenced our thinking on this work. We feel lucky to work with so many dedicated colleagues who are also thinking about this important topic.

We thank the staff, students, and communities of Dublin City Schools and the Parkway School District, who have been extremely supportive of our work and of our professional growth. We both feel fortunate to work in school districts that are committed to students in this ever-changing digital age. Each day we learn from our students, and we feel lucky to have administrators and colleagues who push us to stay grounded in our work with children.

As the foundation of much of our professional learning, NCTE has provided integral development for both of us. When we met as members of the Executive Committee several years ago, we were encouraged to think beyond our current realities as we helped to develop the *NCTE Framework for 21st Century Curriculum and Assessment*. Special thanks to Kathy Yancey, Kylene Beers, Kent Williamson, and those we served with on the Executive Committee for leading us through this process and allowing us to see beyond 2008.

The entire editorial staff at NCTE has been supportive of our work and our process. Writing a book as part of the Principles in Practice imprint has been a great opportunity. Working with imprint editor Cathy Fleischer pushed our thinking and helped us to ask ourselves questions we hadn't considered. The book could not have been written without her time, energy, and knowledge of sound literacy practice. We also appreciate the collaborative support we received from Troy Hicks and Kristen Turner as they were writing their own book for this strand of Reading in Today's Classrooms.

Finally, we want to thank our families, who patiently endured through the many hours of Google Hangouts, phone calls, and computer time that took us away from daily life. To Scott Sibberson and Kim Bass, for their support through this entire process. They both understand the importance of this topic and our commitment to it. And to our children—Maxwell and Molly Bass; Alexa and Ana Sibberson—who have grown up in this digital age and don't find the technology special but, rather, simply part of who they are.

Reading Instruction for *All* Students

An NCTE Policy Research Brief

Reading instruction has always been stressed for elementary school students, but today it takes on increased importance for *all* grades. Reports like *Time to Act* and *Reading at Risk* raise concern about a lack of depth in the literacy education of adolescent students and lament a general decline in reading among young adults. The Common Core State Standards (CCSS) for reading state that "all students must be able to comprehend texts of steadily increasing complexity as they progress through school," and studies of literacy point to the rising expectations for reading in both schooling and the workplace.[1] Documents like these indicate that teachers need to help all students become readers, regardless of whether they are in elementary or secondary school, so they can succeed in the information age.

Two terms are circulating in current discussions of reading instruction: textual complexity and close reading. Textual complexity is defined in the CCSS as a three-part entity. It includes *quantitative dimensions* such as word length or frequency, sentence length, and cohesion, all of which can be measured by computer software; *qualitative dimensions* such as levels of meaning, clarity of language, and knowledge demands, all of which require human readers; and *reader-text variables* such as reader motivation, knowledge, and experience, qualities best assessed by teachers who know students and texts.[2] Both the qualitative dimensions and the reader-text variables depend upon the professional judgment of teachers, especially the reader-text variables, because only teachers know students well enough to help them find the best text for the purpose at hand, something "leveling" systems cannot do. Research on student readers and the texts they read confirms the need for teachers to play a key role in matching individual students with specific books at appropriate levels of textual complexity:

What we know about our students as readers:

- Students come to reading tasks with varied prior reading experiences, or prior knowledge, which can support their reading of complex texts.
- Students who are engaged and motivated readers read more often and read more diverse texts than students who are unmotivated by the reading task.
- Students who develop expertise with a particular kind of reading—science fiction or online games, for example—outside of school may not think this kind of reading will be valued by their teachers.[3]

What we know about the texts students read:

- In and out of school, the texts students read vary significantly, from linear text-only books to multimodal textbooks to online hypertexts, each of which places different demands on readers and requires different strategies and approaches to reading.
- Students read texts from a variety of disciplines, so content area literacy is important.

Reading Instruction for *All* Students

- The level of difficulty or complexity in a text is not the only factor students consider in choosing texts; interest and motivation also matter.
- Readability or lexile levels can vary significantly within a single text, so it is important to consider other dimensions of textual complexity.[4]

Close reading has been proposed as the way to help students become effective readers of complex texts, and it can be useful, especially when used alongside other approaches. The difficulty is that close reading can be defined in multiple terms. It can mean searching for hidden meanings, positioning the text as the only reality to be considered, and focusing on formal features. Close reading is also a highly contested term among college English instructors. Critics condemn it for conceptualizing the text as a closed world, for limiting student access, and for emphasizing form over content.[5]

Furthermore, research shows that reading comprehension depends on a more complex approach. Specifically, reading comprehension results from the integration of two models, text-based and situation-based. The text-based model focuses on the way words are organized into sentences, paragraphs, and whole texts. The situation model refers to the meaning that results from integration of the text-based approach with the reader's prior knowledge and goals. Close reading is aligned with the text-based approach, and it encourages students to see meaning as one right answer to be extracted from the text. Close reading is often conflated with providing textual evidence for making a claim about a text, but any approach to reading can insist on warrants for interpretations of texts. By itself, then, close reading cannot ensure that students will develop deep understandings of what they read.[6]

Implications for Instructional Policy

Research-based understandings about students, texts, and reading underlie instructional approaches that support students' learning to read complex texts across grade levels and disciplines. Policymakers need to affirm the value of multiple approaches and support teachers' efforts to adopt instructional practices that call upon a variety of effective strategies, including the following.

- Recognize the role that motivation plays in students' reading by modeling for students how to engage with complex texts that do and do not interest them.
- Engage students in performative reading responses such as gesture, mime, vocal intonation, characterization, and dramatization to enable active construction of meaning and construct a collaborative environment that builds on the strengths of individual students.
- Have students read multiple texts focused on the same topic to improve comprehension through text-to-text connections.
- Foster students' engagement with complex texts by teaching students how different textual purposes, genres, and modes require different strategies for reading.
- Encourage students to choose texts, including non-fiction, for themselves, in addition to assigned ones, to help them see themselves as capable readers who can independently use reading capabilities they learn in class.

- Demonstrate, especially at the secondary level, how digital and visual texts including multimodal and multigenre texts require different approaches to reading.
- Connect students' reading of complex texts with their writing about reading and with writing that uses complex texts as models so they will recognize and be able to negotiate many different types of complex texts.
- Develop students' ability to engage in meaningful discussion of the complex texts they read in whole-class, small group, and partner conversations so they can learn to negotiate and comprehend complex texts independently.[7]

When teachers can choose from a range of research-based and theoretically grounded instructional approaches, their students learn how to choose from, apply, and reflect on diverse strategies as they take up the varied purposes, subjects, and genres that present complex challenges for readers. Publishers, as well as policymakers and administrators, play an important role in assuring that teachers have appropriate texts and materials to support effective instruction.

Implications for Policies on Formative Assessment

Research shows that formative assessment enables teachers to draw on their knowledge of the students in their classes in order to adjust instruction over time. Accordingly, educational policy needs to affirm the importance of high-quality formative assessment in reading instruction.[8] Formative assessment of reading can take many forms, as the examples below show:

- Teachers can help students develop awareness of their diverse experiences and knowledge—all of which affect the ways they engage with texts. These include reading experiences in previous grades and in out-of-school spaces. Once students have identified their experiences and knowledge, teachers can help students build on them in approaching complex texts—including when their background experiences and knowledge enhance and/or interfere with their ability to read complex texts.
- Asking students to think aloud as they read complex texts can help teachers identify which instructional supports and interventions will best support readers as they face new reading challenges.
- When teachers have identified students who struggle to remain engaged as they read complex texts, they can assess students' interests in order to provide texts that are more likely to foster student engagement.
- Teachers can assess students' ability to think about their reading and about how different kinds of texts impact their reading. This increased awareness can improve students' ability to read complex texts for various purposes.[9]

Implications for Policies on Professional Learning for Teachers

Reading research shows that educational policy needs to include professional development opportunities that enable teachers to match instructional approaches to diverse

Reading Instruction for *All* Students

student needs. In order to support teachers' ability to draw on a complex set of instructional approaches in service of diverse learner reading outcomes, teachers need frequent and sustained opportunities to learn with one another about the range of instructional supports, interventions, and formative assessments as they emerge from the latest reading research and practice. Opportunities to deepen understanding of topics like those listed below will prepare teachers to help students meet the challenges of textual complexity:

- Broaden the repertoire of approaches to reading instruction, drawing on recent and authenticated research.
- Deepen understanding of which combinations of reading strategies are most effective for achieving a particular instructional goal or addressing the needs of a particular student.
- Learn about how disciplinary distinctions open opportunities and challenges for teaching students to read for varied purposes.
- Develop insight into which reading strategies are effective in all disciplines and which are uniquely suited to specific fields.[10]

Preparing students to read complex texts effectively is one of the most important and most challenging responsibilities of schools. With research-based support from policymakers and administration, teachers can enable students at all grade levels to comprehend, draw evidence from, and compare across a wide variety of complex texts.

Endnotes

1. Carnegie Council on Advancing Adolescent Literacy. (2010). *Time to act: An agenda for advancing adolescent literacy for college and career success.* New York, NY: Carnegie Corporation of New York.

National Endowment for the Arts. (2004). *Reading at risk: A survey of literary reading in America.* Washington, DC: Research Division, National Endowment for the Arts.

Common Core State Standards for English Language Arts & Literacy in History/Social Studies, Science, and Technical Subjects, p. 4. http://www.corestandards.org/assets/CCSSI_ ELA%20Standards.pdf.

2. Common Core State Standards for English Language Arts & Literacy in History/Social Studies, Science, and Technical Subjects. Appendix A: Research supporting key elements of the standards. Glossary of key terms. http://www.corestandards.org/assets/Appendix_A.pdf.

3. McNamara, D. S., Kintsch, E., Songer, N. B., & Kintsch, W. (1996). Are good texts always better? Text coherence, background knowledge, and levels of understanding in learning from text. *Cognition and Instruction, 14,* 1–43.

Venable, G. P. (2003). Confronting complex text: Readability lessons from students with language learning disabilities. *Topics in Language Disorders, 23*(3), 225–240.

Brozo, W. G., Shiel, G., & Topping, K. (2007). Engagement in reading: Lessons learned from three PISA countries. *Journal of Adolescent & Adult Literacy, 51*(4), 304–315.

Kajder, S. (2010). *Adolescents and digital literacies: Learning alongside our students.* Urbana, IL: National Council of Teachers of English.

4. Hayles, N. K. (2010). How we read: Close, hyper, machine. *ADE Bulletin, 22*(150), 62–79.

Foorman, B. R., Francis, D. J., Davidson, K. C., Harm, M. W., & Griffin, J. (2009). Variability in text features in six grade 1 basal reading programs. *Scientific Studies of Reading 8* (2), 167–197.

Pitcher, B., & Fang, Z. (2007). Can we trust leveled texts? An examination of their reliability and quality from a linguistic perspective. *Literacy, 41*, 43–51.

5. Student Achievement Partners. Guidelines for developing text-dependent questions for close analytical reading. http:// www.achievethecore.org/steal-these-tools/text-dependent-questions.

Bialostosky, D. (2006). Should college English be close reading? *College English, 69*(2), 111–116.

Murray, H. (1991). Close reading, closed writing. *College English 53*(2), 195–208.

Rabinowitz, P. J. (1992). Against close reading. *Pedagogy Is Politics.* Ed. Maria-Regina Kecht. Chicago: University of Illinois Press.

6. Kintsch, W. (1988). The role of knowledge in discourse comprehension: A construction-integration model. *Psychological Review, 95*, 163–182.

7. Adomat, D. S. (2010). Dramatic interpretations: Performative responses of young children to picture book read-alouds. *Children's Literature in Education, 41*(3), 207–221.

Brozo et al. (2007).

Coiro, J. (2011). Talking about reading as thinking: Modeling the hidden complexities of online reading comprehension. *Theory into Practice 50*(2), 107.

Hayles (2010).

Hiebert, E. H. (2011). The Common Core's staircase of text complexity: Getting the size of the first step right. *Reading Today, 29*(3), 26–27.

Heisey, N., & Kucan, L. (2010). Introducing science concepts to primary students through read-alouds: Interactions and multiple texts make the difference. *The Reading Teacher, 63*(8), 666–676.

Juzwik, M. M., Nystrand, M., Kelly, S., & Sherry, M. B. (2008). Oral narrative genres as dialogic resources for classroom literature study: A contextualized case study of conversational narrative discussion. *American Educational Research Journal, 45*(4), 1111–1154.

Palincsar, A. S., & Schutz, K. M. (2011): Reconnecting strategy instruction with its theoretical roots, *Theory into Practice, 50*(2), 85–92.

Pike, M. M., Barnes, M. A., & Barron, R. W. (2010). The role of illustrations in children's inferential comprehension. *Journal of Experimental Child Psychology, 105*(3).

Quirk, M., Schwanenflugel, P. J., & Webb, M. Y. (2009). A short-term longitudinal study of the relationship between motivation to read and reading fluency skill in second grade. *Journal of Literacy Research, 41*(2).

Tunks, K. W. (2011). Exploring journals as a genre for making reading–writing connections. *Childhood Education, 87*(3), 169.

8. NCTE. (2010). Fostering high-quality formative assessment: A policy brief produced by the National Council of Teachers of English. *The Council Chronicle, 20*(1), 12–15.

Reading Instruction for *All* Students

9. Brown, C. L. (2007). Supporting English language learners in content-reading. *Reading Improvement, 44*(1).

Caldwell, J., & Leslie, L. (2010). Thinking aloud in expository text: Processes and outcomes. *Journal of Literacy Research, 42*(3), 308–340.

Collins, P., Land, R. E., Pearson, M., et al. (2012). Enhancing the interpretive reading and analytical writing of mainstreamed English learners in secondary school: Results from a randomized field trial using a cognitive strategies approach. *American Educational Research Journal, 49*(2), 323–355.

Horning, A. S. (2011). Where to put the manicules: A theory of expert reading. *Across the Disciplines, 8*(2). http://wac.colostate. edu/atd/articles/horning2011/index.cfm.

Little, C. A., & Hines, A. H. (2006). Time to read: Advancing reading achievement after school. *Journal of Advanced Academics, 18*(1), 8–33.

McNamara et al. (1996).

Ramsay, C. M., & Sperling, R. A. (2010). Designating reader perspective to increase comprehension and interest. *Contemporary Educational Psychology, 35*(3), 215–227.

Venable (2003).

10. Herman, J., Hanson, T. L., Boscardin, C. K., et al. (2011). Integrating literacy and science in biology: Teaching and learning impacts of reading apprenticeship professional development. *American Educational Research Journal 48*(3).

Liang, L. A. (2011). Scaffolding middle school students' comprehension and response to short stories. *Research in Middle Level Education Online, 34*(8), 1–16. http://www.nmsa.org/Publications/RMLEOnline/Articles/Vol34No8/tabid/2405/Default. aspx.

This policy brief was produced by NCTE's James R. Squire Office of Policy Research, directed by Anne Ruggles Gere, with assistance from Anne Beatty Martinez, Elizabeth Homan, Danielle Lillge, Justine Neiderhiser, Chris Parsons, Ruth Anna Spooner, Sarah Swofford, and Chinyere Uzogara.

Defining Digital Reading

Building an identity means coming to see in ourselves the characteristics of particular categories (and roles) of people and developing a sense of what it feels like to be that sort of person and belong in certain social situations.

—*Choice Words*, Peter Johnston

Looking up from a reading conference to check in on how the class was doing during independent reading time, I (Franki) noticed two third-grade girls, Julia and Marissa, sitting side by side staring intently at their laptops, each having chosen to read online content for their day's reading. From afar, it looked as though both girls were engaged digital readers. They were focused on the screen, clicking around, seeming to know what they were doing—proficient in their ability to interact with this form of text. Five years ago I might have been satisfied with this scene, but recently I have come to learn that merely reading on a computer does not make a digital reader. From a distance, these two girls look to have similar skills, but when I take a closer look at their reading habits, I can identify big differences.

Watching Julia over time, I would identify her as a strong reader in this digital age because of her habits with a variety of texts. She owns a Kindle Fire and is intentional in her decisions about when she will read a book on her Kindle rather than in its traditional print form. Julia is willing to take risks when it comes to her reading, whether she is reading digitally or traditionally. She tries new genres, explores new tools, and works through any confusions. She is equally comfortable struggling with understandings in a longer print novel as she is with an online nonfiction article. I often see her sitting with an iPad in one hand and a dry-erase board or notebook in the other as she consistently finds the tools she needs to meet her purposes and shows flexibility in her choice of tool. She moves between traditional and digital devices with an ease that makes the device she chooses secondary to her goals as a reader. When reading online, Julia is intentional about deciding when to hit a link and further explore a topic and when to skip the link and just read on. In addition, Julia constantly shares her life as a reader and as a learner with me and her classmates, and the posts she composes on her Kidblogs blog are well crafted because she has spent time reading many blogs and learning from other writers—in other words, her online reading greatly influences her own writing. She regularly talks about what she reads, is always looking for new ways to capture her thinking, and, as she shows in her conversation and blog posts, is reflective about her reading life. She is part of a community of readers, and because of that she learns from others in order to grow herself.

Marissa, on the other hand, merely imitates many of Julia's behaviors. She *looks* like she knows what she is doing when she reads digitally, but with a closer look, I realize there is no intentionality. She randomly bops around the Internet, playing a game or skimming an article, but she doesn't seem to have a plan for where to go or a clear purpose when she is on a digital device. She doesn't seem to synthesize and think across texts, but she is clearly enamored with the technology. She has her own iPad and often carries it around so that she has immediate access to text, but she is unwilling to grab hold of a text and dig into it; rather, she interacts with most texts at a superficial level. Unlike Julia, Marissa is not intentional in her reading choices and often reads the most popular thing in the classroom at the time. She struggles in most areas, including comprehension, decoding, and stamina, regardless of the text, but because she uses the technology of the day, her classmates tend to see her as a fairly strong digital reader.

Julia and Marissa are very different in their approach to reading in the digital age. One has strong reading habits whereas the other disguises her habits as she imitates the actions of her classmates. One is flexible in her approach to a variety of texts whereas the other is more fixed in her habits. One is willing to take risks in her reading whereas the other chooses what is convenient and comfortable.

These two students are at different points in their reading journey, but both are influenced by the digital tools of the day. Their experiences point to the kinds of questions that teachers across the country are facing: How do we move students who are surface-level readers like Marissa to adopt the deeper reading habits of students like Julia? How do the reading skills and strategies that we've taught for years translate into a world and classroom where technology is as much a part of the culture as paper and pencil? These are questions that the two of us, a long-time elementary teacher (Franki Sibberson) and a district technology coordinator and former high school English teacher (Bill Bass), have focused on over the past several years. We explore these questions and others throughout these pages as we consider the implications of what it takes for students like Julia and Marissa to navigate reading in the digital age.

What Do We Know about Reading?

As we attempt to answer these questions, we must return to what we know to be true about reading and reading instruction. In 2012, NCTE released the *Reading Instruction for All Students* policy research brief, recognizing and helping to shape the current reality of reading in our schools. Through this brief, we are reminded that it's as important as ever for us to continue to match students with books that will help them to be successful and grow as readers, especially as the texts that students are reading continue to expand in scope and medium.

Along this same vein, the brief reminds us that it is important that we continue to recognize what years of research into reading and reading instruction tell us about our students as readers—even as we move into the digital age. As the policy brief states, we already know some significant things:

- Students come to reading tasks with varied prior reading experiences, or prior knowledge, which can support their reading of complex texts.
- Students who are engaged and motivated readers read more often and read more diverse texts than students who are unmotivated by the reading task.
- Students who develop expertise with a particular kind of reading—science fiction or online games, for example—outside of school may not think this kind of reading will be valued by their teachers. (NCTE, *Reading* ix; all page numbers for the research brief map to the version printed at the front of this book)

Each of these points gives us some insight into the reading lives of our students, but they can also challenge us as we think beyond the printed text and into the digital. How do these understandings of students as readers transfer to students who are reading in the digital age? How does it help us to know that our students' "prior reading experiences" include broad and multiple experiences with online reading? How does digital reading impact student engagement and motivation? And does the particular expertise students develop in their out-of-school digital reading have a place in schools? Julia's reading habits, in particular, can give us insight: Julia is adept at moving between mediums and choosing her reading mode based on her reading goals. This comes with the experience of being introduced and encouraged to read various types of texts and calls on her prior experience to support her reading tasks. She is also a motivated reader who chooses texts that challenge her and push her thinking and reading skills. Finally, Julia is experienced with reading online texts, such as blogs, and sees them as a part of her reading life.

As we teachers look at the experiences of our own Julias and Marissas, we can see the many challenges in this shift to digital reading that we must recognize and address. Digital reading experiences must be a part of the opportunities we give students on a regular basis. If not, we're discounting much of the reading they will engage with in the future.

Bridging the Home and School Gap with Digital Reading

In October of 2013, Bill sat in on a number of student focus groups covering grades 3–12 convened to look at the role of technology in both their lives and their education. Their thoughts were not surprising: each group identified technology and the Internet as crucial for their current understanding and future work.

One student, Sara, recounted her experiences in the classroom and elaborated on feeling that school is leaving her ill prepared for her future challenges. Sara is an eighth grader who isn't doing particularly well in school. She has too many absences and doesn't always do her work, but according to both her and her teachers, her behavior is good, so, as she says, "adults leave me alone." Sara comes to school and "powers down." While students are allowed to bring their devices to school thanks to the district Bring Your Own Device (BYOD) program, none of her teachers allows student devices to be used in class because "they can't tell what we're doing on them and they don't trust us. Instead we have to use these old desktop and laptop computers the school gives us." This is a big deal for Sara, who, while acknowledging that not everyone will be responsible with technology and that many of her classmates have made poor choices, feels punished even though she hasn't broken that trust. For her, a big part of the disconnect between in-school and out-of-school literacies is simply access. She's an avid reader but most of her reading is done in ebooks and online—except when she's in school. At school she is distant because the class content seems stale. She is forced to read linearly rather than exploring what she's reading and making her own connections through the hyperlinked texts and multimedia of the Web. "If only I could get my phone or iPad out. Given ten minutes, I could find all the information in the textbook and more. I can answer any question they ask because all [the questions] require is a Google search." Sara's final appeal to teachers arises from the research projects she does in class:

> The research that I have to do is completely contrived and is always on a topic that my teacher gives me. We go to the library, log in to the computers, and have exactly ninety minutes to gather all our research and then go write a paper. That doesn't give me enough time to really understand the topic. So what I do is just find my three sources or whatever my teacher wants, regurgitate some information, and then turn it in. I really don't know if he even reads it. What it comes down to is that my research in school is just going through the motions. I know that I do research every day, not just during the one or two class periods that my teacher can get us in the computer lab.

Sara's story isn't unique. She feels disconnected from her learning and her reading. She doesn't see the connections between her school and home reading lives because either the school readings lack intentionality or her teachers haven't fully made the connections for her. Her parting words as she left the focus group were, "I know school is important and I want to do well because that's what everyone expects of me. But if I really want to learn something, I do that outside of school."

The Changing Face of Literacy

Over the past five years, the world of technology has exploded, and as part of that explosion, everything connected to technology seems to be termed a *literacy*. Whether we're talking about digital literacy, information literacy, Web literacy, or tech literacy, we notice that all of these terms have one idea in common: literacy. So what does it actually mean to be literate in the digital age? What elements are common among all these literacies that we, as educators, can draw from and work with in a meaningful way? And how do we determine which of these elements are worth focusing on in our teaching and which we should ignore? (Because, let's face it, as teachers we know that every attempt to try something new in our classroom means we have to let something else go.) So how do we decide whether any new thing—especially any new thing concerning technology—has enough potential to try? How do we determine the best ways to use technology in order to teach reading in a digital age?

These questions and many others are also intrinsic to NCTE's *Reading Instruction for* All *Students* policy research brief, especially in its opening statement: "Reading instruction has always been stressed for elementary school students, but today it takes on increased importance for *all* grades. Reports like *Time to Act* and *Reading at Risk* raise concern about a lack of depth in the literacy education of adolescent students and lament a general decline in reading among young adults" (ix). Literacy instruction is paramount to the success of our students, yet we still struggle with low literacy rates and questions about how to best prepare students for a world that hasn't yet been invented.

Increasing literacy rates, increasing the amount of reading students do, preparing students for a world that hasn't yet been invented—these are the dilemmas that literacy teachers face every single day. Layering on top of these dilemmas the multitude of digital tools available and waiting to be tried makes it all the more important for teachers to understand and articulate what our core beliefs are about literacy instruction and to remain true to them. As two experienced literacy educators, we believe we need to meet students in the digital world in which they live, but we need to do so in a way that is not solely about the technology. We need to find ways to encourage more students to become more like Julia, who uses technology as one of many tools toward becoming a flexible and competent reader, rather than remaining like Marissa, who perhaps sees the glitter of technology but doesn't necessarily know how to use it to become a competent reader.

A starting point for this work is to define what digital literacy actually is, and what it's not. In 2008 the NCTE Executive Committee created a definition of *21st century literacies* (see Figure 1.1) that helped to harness the idea that the digital age is upon us and to give educators direction for literacy instruction. Updated in 2013, this definition does not focus on technology as the driving force behind literacy, nor does it equate the two. What it does is create a distinct connection between the world of literacy and that of technology and digital age skills. This connection is not one that teachers can ignore.

Again, one of the things this definition does not do (which we firmly condone) is suggest that technology equals digital literacy. Just because students are "good" with technology does not necessarily mean they are literate in the digital age. Digital literacy is much more than that. As we work with students in the classroom, it's clear that students in grades 3–8 have spent a lot of time with technology. It's a part of them and their existence. As is often said, this generation has never known a world without computers, smartphones, and high-speed Internet. But even though they've internalized how to use technology, too many students still use it on a superficial level. They may know where their games are bookmarked or where their app folder is on a device, but they aren't necessarily digitally literate. This knowledge makes them technology users but certainly doesn't give them a deep understanding of how the tools work, what the best tool might be for a specific task, or even what other tools might be available—skills that are vital to becoming truly literate. It takes time and experience to become a true digital reader, to figure out where and when particular tools fit into the reading process; and as we've learned, there are plenty of traps along the way. In this book, we explore the experiences digital readers must have to be able to navigate the digital texts they will encounter, as well as the kinds of lessons teachers today must develop.

Figure 1.1. *The NCTE Definition of 21st Century Literacies.*

Literacy has always been a collection of cultural and communicative practices shared among members of particular groups. As society and technology change, so does literacy. Because technology has increased the intensity and complexity of literate environments, the 21st century demands that a literate person possess a wide range of abilities and competencies, many literacies. These literacies are multiple, dynamic, and malleable. As in the past, they are inextricably linked with particular histories, life possibilities, and social trajectories of individuals and groups. Active, successful participants in this 21st century global society must be able to

- Develop proficiency and fluency with the tools of technology;
- Build intentional cross-cultural connections and relationships with others so [as] to pose and solve problems collaboratively and strengthen independent thought;
- Design and share information for global communities to meet a variety of purposes;
- Manage, analyze, and synthesize multiple streams of simultaneous information;
- Create, critique, analyze, and evaluate multimedia texts;
- Attend to the ethical responsibilities required by these complex environments.

What Is Digital Reading?

As our understanding of digital literacy has evolved, it only makes sense that what we define as *digital reading* also evolves. But here's the dilemma: Teachers who have immersed themselves for many years in best practices research surrounding reading instruction and who have worked hard to create successful classroom experiences for children already have a good understanding of what it takes to teach someone to read and how to use research-based practices to inform reading instruction. For many teachers, connecting these deep understandings with current changes in technology creates a challenge. How do we help teachers keep true to what we know about the best ways of teaching students to read *and* introduce digital reading into the mix?

We agree with Kylene Beers and Robert Probst's statement about reading in their book *Notice and Note: Strategies for Close Reading*: "The most rigorous reading is to find what those words on that page mean in our own lives" (42). We know this has always been true of all reading, and in this digital age, helping students find the meaning in their own lives becomes even more important. For our students to experience a reading life in which reading changes who they are and thus changes their worlds, our definition of reading in the classroom must expand. Although reading in the digital age still includes reading powerful novels, it must also include digital pieces and digital tools.

One thing we do know: we can't view digital reading as an add-on; in other words, we can't wait until a child is competent with traditional literacy skills and then expect the child to transfer those skills to digital text. It's not quite that easy. While there are clear overlaps between digital and traditional reading instruction, students also need specific experiences if they are to effectively navigate all types of texts and be active digital readers. If we focus only on traditional texts—or on traditional texts first—students will not magically develop these skills. Such skills must be fostered and taught, just as we foster and teach traditional strategies and skills (see Figure 1.2).

We believe that digital reading is a complex idea that has changed the way we interact with various texts. Unfortunately, digital reading is often defined in a narrow way that focuses on format of the text and *what* is being read. For example, Dalton and Proctor have identified four types of digital texts:

- *linear text in digital format*—ebooks and many PDFs are examples of this type of text in which the print version is simply made digital

- *nonlinear text with hyperlinks*—most webpages and blogs and text with links fall into this category

- *texts with integrated media*—another type of nonlinear text that includes video, audio, and interactive pieces to support the message of the work

- *texts with response options*—an invitation to join a discussion outside of the text in a discussion forum or other online community (300)

Although we agree that many examples of digital reading fall into one of these categories, we believe that digital reading is more than merely reading various types of digital text. The work of Dalton and Proctor has helped us begin to think about ways in which reading is changing, but we find the behaviors around these new texts to be most important. We don't want our students merely to be able to read and understand nonlinear texts. Instead, we want them to be intentional about

Figure 1.2. What digital reading is and isn't.

Digital Reading IS	Digital Reading IS NOT
ongoing and embedded	a one-time event
about understanding	about the technology
active	passive
intentional	random
flexible	linear
about choice	the same experience for everyone

when and how to choose which types of texts will help them find and best understand the message and medium. By helping students to recognize the types of texts they will encounter and how to interact with these various kinds of texts, they will gain independence in their reading choices and have more autonomy in their reading lives.

Figure 1.3 lists the skills—based in traditional reading—that we want our students to have if they are to be active digital readers.

Think back for a moment to the description of Julia's reading habits at the beginning of this chapter and you can see that she demonstrates many of the traditional skills that make her an effective reader of any kind of text. She can move easily between text types, and she is willing to try various strategies until she finds one that works. Marissa is not as comfortable with these skills, and so our teaching must support her in developing these.

We continue to recognize that reading in the digital age is not without its challenges. Bill, for example, in his role as a technology coordinator who works with teachers, sees them struggle with bringing digital reading into their classrooms. Gretchen Morrison, an instructional coach and teacher at Highcroft Ridge Elementary School in Chesterfield, Missouri, recently described one of the challenges she regularly faces when conferencing with students:

> With a regular book, when I approach a student who is reading, I can immediately tell what part of the book they are currently working on simply by what page they are on. That visual cue helps me to know what questions I should be asking and where to begin my conference. With a digital text, I don't have that visual cue. I can get around it, but it takes a shift in thinking on the part of the teacher.

This dilemma of finding a new way to easily identify a student's progress with a book is just one hands-on example of an issue teachers need to consider as they work with students on their reading in digital formats. And while it may take a shift in thinking, it's a shift that can't be avoided. Instead, we must embrace the options that are now available and see the possibilities that exist because of the variety of texts students now have access to.

Why Focus on Grades 3–8? The Possibilities and Challenges

Grades 3–8 are critical years for readers. Our students are moving from being emergent readers to becoming transitional readers and finally independent readers. Traditionally in these grades, our students move from reading picture books and early chapter books to reading more complex texts across content areas. This stage of literacy is critical as students build on their early experiences to become more sophisticated readers.

Figure 1.3. How digital reading expands traditional reading skills.

Skill We've Always Taught	Ways These Skills Expand and Change Because of Digital Tools
Annotating	• Ebooks have embedded tools for annotation and note taking. • Several note-taking apps make connecting annotations between multiple books and readers more accessible. • Various tools allow readers to organize and reorganize ideas as their thinking grows and changes across a text.
Reading across texts	• Links within texts create connections between various texts and media elements. • Numerous tools allow readers to bookmark or create collections of sites around reader-defined categories.
Determining importance	• New digital tools are not always linear, creating a variety of distractions for readers and making determining importance of a text and a source a more complex skill.
Connecting and synthesizing	• E-readers allow readers to see annotations and lines highlighted by other readers. • Social networking allows readers to connect with authors, publishers. and readers across the globe.
Monitoring comprehension	• Clicking and skipping around is easy with many forms of digital texts, so it's more important than ever that students learn how to monitor for comprehension.
Repairing meaning	• Skimming and scanning becomes more difficult with visual and audio distractions on online resources. • A variety of sources are immediately at a reader's fingertips and can be used to build and repair meaning. • Readers must be intentional and know when to use links and connected resources for better understanding.
Knowing where to go	• The many resources means students need to gain familiarity with a variety of tools and sources of information in order to find resources. • Students need to understand the strengths and limitations of each source. • Students need to understand how to determine whether source and information are credible and authentic.
Asking questions	• Readers must go beyond the kind of fact finding and trivia finding made easy by technology in order to dig deeply for answers to questions. • Students can move forward in a reading journey more easily as so many sources are available quickly.
Sharing in multiple ways	• Students and teachers can choose tools for sharing that make sense for purpose and audience. • The possibility for authentic audience expands with the ease of sharing. • Using the right tool to share information most effectively becomes more difficult as the number of tools increases.
Changing thinking	• The amount of available information is endless, so readers must constantly add new learning to their understanding and change their thinking.

We believe strongly that students in grades 3–8 have unique needs as learners and that by the time students get to high school, they have already developed a *stance* toward literacy and attitudes about the role technology can play in their lives. While we are not suggesting that it's too late for these older students, their prior experiences with digital tools and texts have already shaped their understanding of the role these play in their lives as learners. As teachers of students in grades 3–8, we have the ability to influence these attitudes and set the stage for students' future success as digital readers.

Between the ages of eight and fourteen, kids find their voices and move toward independence as readers, writers, and learners. In addition, thirteen is considered the "golden age" for children when it comes to digital literacy and online tools—the age at which children can create their own accounts and officially become part of the online world that many adults take for granted. Before students turn thirteen, then, we want them to be independent users of digital tools. To get them there, we have to scaffold that usage in different ways. At the secondary level, many kids are already using a number of digital tools and experimenting on their own, but in third grade, very few children use these tools for the purpose of learning. We have found that they may dabble in educational games their parents have bookmarked in a browser or downloaded to a tablet, but the direct connection between these tools and the process of learning is often foreign to them.

As educators in grades 3–8, we know that our role in schools is to support our students' literacy by helping them intentionally use digital tools for learning and make these tools a part of their daily lives. We do this by being intentional about our own work with students so that they can enter high school and college with a stronger stance as learners who understand the power of digital tools in their own reading, writing, and learning.

Students will not learn to be successful and independent readers of digital texts with just one lesson or one set of lessons. Rather, learning to read digital texts must be *embedded* in the ways we do our literacy work on a day-to-day basis. Just as we know that students come into the classroom with a variety of reading experiences, we know that they come with a variety of experiences in the digital world. We can't assume that because they are growing up in a time when digital tools permeate their lives, they already know how and when to use these tools and which tools to select based on their need. This means that educators must go beyond creating a lesson or unit on digital reading, digital citizenship, or digital literacy. Instead, the processes and tools must be a part of the work that teachers and students do on a regular basis, not an add-on to a lesson or a reward for behavior or a job well done on an assessment.

It is also in grades 3–8 that our students move to more complex texts. Grades K–2 focus on emergent literacy as students are beginning to read, whereas in grades 3–8 they begin to read texts with more complexity and sophistication. As they make that transition, students need to learn a number of new skills, even if they are competent readers in grades K–2. As Franki and Karen Szymusiak wrote in *Still Learning to Read*,

> Our older readers still have much to learn about reading. It makes sense that students in grades 3–6 need more instruction. The texts they are reading are becoming much more complex and sophisticated. As readers, they will be asked to think through complex themes, analyze characters, and respond at higher levels. For these students to grow as readers, they need more instruction. We can't assume that the skills our students learned in grades K–2 will carry them through their lives as readers. They are ready for new skills and more independence. (2)

We think this statement is as true today as it was ten years ago—and certainly applies to teaching students to read in the digital age. We certainly cannot "teach" students to read every format and medium available. But it is important to stay true to what we know about good literacy teaching: teaching that teaches the reader, not the text. This is especially critical with digital reading so that students can transfer skills to whatever new forms of texts are introduced, regardless of medium.

Why Does Digital Reading Matter in Grades 3–8?

Years ago, during the Harry Potter craze, many very young children were reading the Harry Potter books. It seemed that every time either of us went to a family function or a neighborhood gathering, we'd hear about a seven-year-old who was "just loving" Harry Potter. This concerned us because so many of the nuances of the Harry Potter books seem beyond a seven-year-old's life experiences. We are confident that these seven-year-olds could read the words in the Harry Potter books, probably fluently. And we're sure that these children had an understanding of the basic plot of the books. But the books are complex, and complex texts consist of more layers to understanding than mere plot. While we worry a bit that these students were missing out on some big ideas that older readers understood, we confess to a bigger worry—about the habits toward reading these young readers were acquiring. We worry that when children read books they can understand only at a surface level, they start expecting only that level of understanding from all their reading; surface-level understanding becomes part of their reading habits. When they always read books that are a stretch for their comprehension level, students find it hard to read closely and to be thoughtful about the text.

We believe the same is true of understanding in all media. We know that our students have literacy experiences at home that involve a variety of media types. Whether these types are online video, electronic games, digital audio files, or even social networking, we know that some children do not have the skills to fully understand what they are reading, watching, playing, or listening to. As with any text-based media, our worry remains the same for these transitional readers: if they continue to read, view, and listen without true understanding, their expectations for meaning are diminished, and they begin to expect that these texts will not always make sense or have meaning. They become passive consumers who read and view in a very simple way. Our worry has been confirmed several times by students who say things like, "We watch videos at home for fun. We don't actually watch them for information. We don't know how to do that!" We want our students to be able to make sense of whatever text they need to make sense of, and we want them to have skills and strategies that work across school and out-of-school literacy experiences.

What to Expect in This Book: A Focus on Three Anchors

Even as we recognize that the text types mentioned earlier (linear texts in digital format, nonlinear texts with hyperlinks, and texts with integrated media) provide some general categories for classifying digital texts, we are more interested in how these texts impact instruction and the needs of students. We believe that what truly matters for classroom practice is bigger than a definition or an activity. What really matters is that our students be engaged in classrooms that focus on *authenticity*, *intentionality*, and *connectedness*. To that end, throughout this book we focus our discussion primarily on these three anchors, emphasizing how they remain the core of digital age workshops as well: *authenticity* (i.e., keeping reading a meaningful experience that extends beyond the classroom), *intentionality* (i.e., making meaningful choices as readers), and *connectedness* (i.e., finding and creating connections between texts, readers, and experiences). Much has been written on these topics, and this book is rooted in the understandings we've gleaned from those who have previously done this work. But as we have thought through these ideas using the lens of instruction in digital literacy, we recognize that each of these anchors requires constant rethinking both as we reimagine their impact through this lens and as we decide where to spend our instructional energy. We ask ourselves daily what matters most within each of these areas and, as we introduce a new tool or strategy, what can we no longer include from our current practice.

Looking back to our two readers, Julia and Marissa, we recognize that we have to think about how to best support all students in a digital reading workshop as they become fluent digital readers. When we talk about digital reading and digital literacy, we are talking about an expanded view of reading and writing. This is not an either/or conversation; we don't want to abandon books completely, and we also don't want to imply that we should access only digital texts. Instead, we want all of our students to be able to read and understand a variety of texts (including digital ones) at high levels. We cannot presume that students must become proficient with traditional texts before we give them opportunities with digital texts. These two mediums must coexist for a well-rounded reader in the digital age. We acknowledge that the processes of reading and writing remain largely the same as they did before the digital age, but digital tools have expanded what is possible as readers and writers. We explore each of these topics more fully in upcoming chapters and make the case that digital work belongs, and can respond, to each of these anchors depending on how we approach them. We also understand that none of these anchors lives on its own and that by addressing one of them, we also address the other two in one fashion or another. If we are intentional about the connections that we help provide and foster for students, there is a far greater chance that students' experiences will be authentic, meaningful, and influential on their reading lives.

In this book, we explore how digital reading might look in the classroom. We also take a look at the ways digital tools have impacted our reading workshops and how we can embed those in an authentic literacy classroom. We have been lucky to learn from a number of teachers in our journey with digital reading, so we have included classroom vignettes from many of these colleagues throughout the book.

From Reading Workshop to Digital Reading Workshop

When are we going to Skype with Lisa Graff?" one of my (Franki's) third-grade students asked a few weeks ago. I was a bit confused as we hadn't planned a Skype visit with this author. "But," Moriya explained, "we finished Lisa Graff's book *The Thing about Georgie* last month in read-aloud and I want to talk to her and ask her some questions. Can't you send her a tweet and see if she can talk to us?"

I was amused at Moriya's assumption that if she wanted to talk to a famous author, it would happen. But mostly I was struck by how much these few sentences said about Moriya as a reader. In this one enthusiastic demand, Moriya let me know that she wanted to talk about a book we had finished as a classroom community, that she knew and loved certain authors, and that she understood the power of being connected. She knew how to get the information she wanted and expected to continue thinking about a book in new ways long after she was finished. I couldn't help but wonder what had made this possible. What was happening in our reading workshop that made all of this a part of who Moriya had become as a reader this year?

In past years, my students have loved reading, had favorite authors, and responded to their reading in a variety of ways, but in this digital age we know there is so much more to being a reader. Still, my reading workshop today looks pretty much the way it did twenty-plus years ago. If you were to walk into my classroom, you would see the walls still lined with bookshelves and the bookshelves still filled with books. There is a big meeting area where students sit for read-aloud, shared reading, mini-lessons, and share sessions. Tables are spread out around the room because while sometimes students like to work alone, other times collaboration is what's called for. In this setting, student choice is critical, and when you walk into our reading workshop, you will see students spread out around the room, reading pieces of their choice.

But though reading workshop *looks* the same, there is a big difference in its inner workings because the digital tools available to readers today actually change what is possible in a workshop. In my classroom today there are iPads and iPods, e-readers and laptops, headphones and a SMART Board. Each of these devices not only provides different reading experiences for my students but also gives us more ways to record our thinking, respond to our reading, and connect with other readers. While no single tool makes *the* difference in the literacy workshop, *collectively* these tools change everything about our teaching and our students' learning.

Why Workshop?

I first read Nancie Atwell's book *In the Middle* years ago over the summer as I was preparing to teach fourth grade for the first time. I had already learned a little bit about reading and writing workshop, but it was Atwell's book that helped me create a vision of what workshop could look like with older elementary students. Nancie Atwell was one of the first to truly define *reading workshop* and to remind us that workshop is about time, ownership, and response.

I immediately began working to set up my classroom and to think through what the workshop would look like when the children arrived. I lined the walls with bookshelves and filled the shelves with books. I wanted my students to be able to choose the books they read, and I wanted them to be part of a community that shared their reading. I spent time making sure we had a class meeting area so that we could talk about our reading lives. Once I had set up the classroom and thought through the routines, I was ready for the kids. As I implemented the reading workshop with actual students, there were—of course—some bumps in the road, but I learned quickly that workshop works. When children are invited to be part of a community and to spend time in school participating in authentic reading activities, they grow in amazing ways. Time, response, and ownership have always been the key pillars for this work as students grow as readers and writers.

Fast-forward twenty-plus years. I believe more strongly than ever that workshop matters and that students still need time, ownership, and response if they are to grow as readers. In that time, though, we've learned so much about reading workshop from experts in the field, and I continue to grow as a teacher every day because of what I've learned from others. Ellin Keene and Susan Zimmermann, for instance, helped to expand my thinking about teaching comprehension strategies through their book, *Mosaic of Thought*. I've thought harder about guided reading groups because of Sharon Taberski's work in *On Solid Ground*, and I've revamped our share sessions to be more powerful because of Leah Mermelstein's *Don't Forget to Share*.

More recently, I read Penny Kittle's *Book Love* and was reminded once again how important time, ownership, and response are as workshop structures. She expands on these ideas and shares classroom practices that support these ideas on her website (www.pennykittle.net) (see Figure 2.1). Over the years, I've tweaked a few things, but the basics of the workshop have remained the same: each day, students read and write, and we come together as a community to study and share and to read independently.

Figure 2.1. Excerpt of Penny Kittle's workshop structure from pennykittle.net.

Time

Students need time to read in class in order to create a habit of reading and set the stage for homework reading, and teachers need reading time to confer individually with students about their choices, stamina, engagement, and goals. Students need time to discuss choices with classmates, time to analyze their progress, and time to practice fluency and comprehension strategies under the direction of the teacher.

Choice

Students need to make choices in reading that reflect their interests because interest drives engagement. Teachers should encourage wide reading in all genres as well as students who pursue an author or genre study. Allow students to reread favorite books and to abandon books that no longer interest them.

Response

Teacher conferences are the primary tool for assessing progress, encouraging goal setting and reflection, and analyzing student needs. Students will reflect on reading in writing (themed notebooks and writing notebooks), facilitate discussions in small groups, join blogs or reading sites for discussions outside of class, and respond regularly to others in the room (Kittle).

Why Digital Reading Workshop?

For years I ignored the technology I was using myself as a reader and writer and didn't consider it something I needed to think about as a teacher. I was committed to reading workshop and the way I was teaching reading workshop because it was working so well—and I felt I couldn't add one more thing (i.e., technology) to our already packed school day. I knew the technology was important, but I didn't think it was a necessity in an elementary classroom. Sure, it was great to do a project here and there, but for the most part, even as my own literacy practices were changing, my classroom workshop remained the same.

At some point during one of my many conversations with Bill, I realized I could no longer ignore the tools of technology. How could I not expand my thinking about workshop when I believed so strongly in authentic literacy experiences for our students and I could see my own reading habits evolve? How could I not rethink workshop when my own definition of what it means to be literate was changing? How could I not rethink workshop when my students were coming to me able to use so many tools and being literate in different ways than they had been just a few years ago?

I began to create a vision for what I wanted my digital reading workshop to look like, but unlike the workshop I implemented after the summer I read Atwell's *In the Middle*, this journey toward change has not been quite as smooth. Every time I figure out how to integrate a new technology idea into my classroom, something changes. Technology is evolving so quickly that it would be easy to jump on the newest tool or gadget without thinking about the bigger picture of literacy. So moving from a traditional reading workshop to a digital reading workshop has been a process. It did not happen overnight and it continues to evolve as I understand more about what it means to be a reader today.

Getting Started with a Digital Reading Workshop

Early in my move toward implementing a digital reading workshop, I realized that although I allowed students to "read" a variety of texts independently during reading workshop, I very seldom used anything other than traditional texts throughout the rest of my instruction. Surprised at this omission, I then created a list of reflective questions to add to my planning notebook as a reminder to really think about the unintentional messages I was sending my students about what "counted" as a "text" in the classroom (see Figure 2.2). By creating this simple list of questions for myself, I was able to plan more thoughtfully and include more types of texts throughout my literacy block. These questions helped me to slow down and become more intentional in my planning and teaching. While it's clear to me that

Figure 2.2. The role of digital texts in the literacy workshop.

What Role Do Digital Texts Play in My Literacy Workshop?

Read-Aloud
- Do I choose to read aloud only texts from traditional books, or do I share digital texts, audio books, blog posts, etc., during read-aloud?
- Do we use Web resources such as author websites and book trailers to help us dig deeper into the book we are reading?
- Do I read aloud from websites and blogs?
- Do I use keyword tags, comments, links, and search features while reading aloud?
- How do we connect with authors whose work we read?
- How do we connect with other classes who are reading/have read the same text?
- How do we track our thinking during read-aloud? Do I rely on easel and chart paper, or do I use a variety of tools such as Notability, Kindle annotations, Corkulous, and other digital tools that help readers respond in different ways to reading?
- Do we connect with the authors of any of the things we read to extend the conversation?

Independent Reading/Reading Conferences
- Do we use online resources for book previewing and book selection?
- Do I limit students' independent reading to traditional books, or do they have a variety of options for their reading time? Do I place equal value on reading on e-readers, reading websites, reading short pieces, etc., as I do on reading traditional books?
- Do I help my students use online tools to support their lives as readers? Do I value annotation tools, bookmarking tools, RSS feeds, etc., as part of my readers' lives? Do I model these tools in mini-lessons?
- Do I introduce digital pieces and discuss digital reading when conferring with students?
- Have I updated my reading interview to include questions about digital reading?
- Do students have ways to add a social component to their lives as readers? Are they connected to others because of their reading?
- Do students have connections inside and outside of the classroom?
- Do students know where to go to find information?
- Are students intentional as readers or are they passive consumers?
- What habits are students developing beyond those of traditional readers?
- Do I value all of the reading that students do both at school and at home?

Reading Mini-Lessons
- Do I use digital text as well as traditional texts when teaching mini-lessons?
- Do I rely completely on traditional text, or do I use film clips, blog entries, podcasts, etc., when planning mini-lessons?
- Do I share process in my mini-lessons? Do I tend to share process only as it relates to creating text-based pieces?
- Do I teach mini-lessons that are universal, regardless of a text's format?
- Do I share my own process, consuming and composing in several types of media?

continued on next page

Figure 2.2. Continued.

- Do I use mini-lesson time to demonstrate tools that support deeper reading with a variety of texts?
- Do my mini-lessons focus on content or also on behaviors and strategies that digital readers have?

Shared Reading
- Have I reflected on the resources I rely on for shared reading?
- Do I include Web reading and viewing when thinking about shared reading experiences?
- How can I include a variety of texts for students to process together?
- What tools do we use in shared experiences?
- How do I model and invite students to try my own reading strategies?

Content Reading
- Have I found sources for content reading that go beyond textbooks and traditional text?
- Do I rely on traditional newspapers for talk about current events, or do I tend to focus more on sites such as DOGOnews, *TIME for Kids,* and other sites that combine text and visual features?
- How am I supporting the importance of visual information in the content areas?
- How do we build understanding across different forms of media?
- How do we connect information to synthesize understanding?

the workshop structures we've always relied on are as important as ever, once I began to embed a variety of tools and texts across my workshop, students began to see digital reading in authentic ways because the technology became a natural part of all they did. Digital reading wasn't an additional part of the classroom; rather, it became integral to the nature of our work. These questions provided the scaffold I needed to be intentional about text choice across all workshop routines and to help my students see the options I had always tried to provide. Throughout the school year, I often find myself returning to this list, and I sometimes add a question or two as I understand more about literacy today. This list keeps me anchored in the effort to expand my workshop in the digital age.

As I reflect on the changes I made as I shifted from a traditional to a digital reading workshop, authenticity seems to be at the center of my thinking. Because the digital tools of the twenty-first century have expanded what we mean by literacy, workshop must change to remain authentic for our students. In Figure 2.3, we identify some of the more obvious differences between a traditional reading workshop and a digital reading workshop. These differences are crucial to creating authentic reading experiences for students. Over time, however, I've come to recognize that the new tools do not change my fundamental beliefs about reading workshop. Lucy Calkins defines reading workshop as a series of reading instruction components that take approximately one hour each class day to complete. Although the order of activities may vary, the daily reading workshop time includes a mini-lesson on a reading strategy, independent reading time, and conferring and coaching time with the teacher. Additionally, the teacher routinely targets small groups of readers who need similar support with specific strategies or guided reading lessons (*The Art of Teacher Reading* 43–44). Calkins's words are as important in a digital reading workshop as they were in a more traditional one.

We have learned again and again that running an authentic reading workshop in this digital age is a huge challenge as we try to keep up with the technology and tools in the midst of teaching children to read. Our classroom days are already

Figure 2.3. Differences between traditional and digital reading workshops.

Reading Workshop	Digital Reading Workshop
Students read independently and with others: both traditional books and magazines	Students read independently: not only traditional books and magazines but also interactive digital text, online sources, websites, ebooks, etc.
The workshop begins with a mini-lesson as a way to bring the class together to learn something new about being a reader.	Mini-lessons have expanded to include a variety of traditional and digital texts and a larger number of skills and strategies.
Share session ends the reading workshop as a way to bring the classroom community together again and to help individuals grow through the sharing.	Sharing still happens at the end of each workshop, but it also happens beyond the classroom walls as students share their reading lives using online tools and social networking sites. Connecting with other classrooms creates a larger community and offers more possibilities for the workshop.
Face-to-face book clubs	Online discussion boards in conjunction with face-to-face conversations
Response—students respond on notebooks, sticky notes, or dry-erase boards.	Students respond in a variety of ways using apps such as Notability, Kindle Annotations, Lino it and Google Docs.
Read-aloud—book and chart	More options are available for read-aloud as students explore various types of text.
Author connections through author visits or letters to authors	Virtual video conferences such as Skype or Google Hangouts

filled with so many mandates and requirements that it is tempting to convince our-selves that all this "digital stuff" is an extra, for kids who already "get it" or for kids who are finished with the *real* work. But we now know better.

Defining the Digital Reading Workshop

Through our journey, we've come to realize that although what it means to be lit-erate has changed, the three basic tenets of a reading workshop—time, ownership, and response—have not. While our ideas about the workshop environment have expanded with all that is possible, our beliefs about how best to support individual readers have remained the same.

But as much as we believe in the foundations of the workshop, we know it isn't enough to run reading workshop just as we always have and to merely include some digital tools. As Troy Hicks reminds us in *The Digital Writing Workshop*, "When we simply bring a traditional mind-set to literacy practices, and not a mind-set that understands new literacies . . . into the process of digital writing, we cannot make the substantive changes to our teaching that need to happen in order to embrace the full potential of collaboration and design that digital writing of-fers" (2). *And we believe that, more than all this, it is the habits and behaviors of readers that define a digital reading workshop.* So as we've changed our mindset about what it means to be a reader today, we've come to believe that the three tenets of time, ownership, and response fall under the umbrella of authenticity.

We know, then, that the structural components of a solid reading workshop that have always been in place should not change:

- Mini-lessons
- Independent reading
- Individual conferences
- Small-group instruction
- Share session and opportunities for response
- Assessment that informs instruction

We've found that a workshop structured in this way helps our students both experience and fall in love with authentic reading. We want our students to be authentic readers and, at the same time, to be intentional, active, and reflective as they read all forms of media. Our workshops are therefore set up with beliefs, routines, and expectations that we hope lead them to live their lives in authentic, intentional, and connected ways. Figure 2.4 lists some questions we ask our stu-dents, questions we push them to begin asking themselves as they live their lives in authentic, intentional, and connected digital reading workshops.

Figure 2.4. Questions for students in a digital reading workshop.

- What tools do you need?
- What decisions do you have to make as a reader?
- How do various tools support you as a reader?
- Which format do you prefer as a reader for this task?
- How do different formats/media support you in different ways?
- Which type of media do you prefer? Why?
- What will you read today?
- What decisions will you make as a reader?
- How and why will you connect with other readers?
- What tools will you use to deepen your understanding about what you read?

At this point in our journey, we believe that digital reading workshop is a structure that believes in young readers. It is a structure that honors authenticity, intentionality, and connectedness. It is a structure that allows each reader to grow and be supported based on individual needs. But, most important, digital reading workshop is a time and place where young readers develop the habits and behaviors they will carry with them throughout their lives. They will learn to be intentional and active readers who know what is possible. It is in our digital reading workshops that our students will learn the power of community, both inside the walls of the classroom and beyond.

Thinking More Deeply about Digital Reading

Being a reader in the digital age is complex and challenging. As we've said, it requires more than transferring traditional reading skills to a new medium. It's about changing the way we think about interacting with ideas and content. It's about giving students opportunities to use the tools as a part of their daily routines and to become independent and flexible in their reading lives. The remainder of this book is organized around our current thinking about what it means to be a reader today and what we believe about digital reading workshop. We further explore the three anchors of authenticity, connectedness, and intentionality and what these mean for classroom instruction. In Chapter 3, we discuss the importance of keeping our reading experiences authentic in the classroom; in Chapter 4, we talk about ways to help our students become intentional decision makers; and in Chapter 5, we explore the power of connectedness and how it relates to our reading lives. Chapter 6 focuses on assessment, and the final chapter discusses the connections between school and home reading. We have been lucky over the past several years to learn from and with several amazing teachers from across the country. We've invited many of these colleagues to share their classroom stories as a way to further expand the possibilities of digital reading with our readers, and their contributions are integrated throughout the book.

What Really Matters? Authenticity

One of my (Franki) favorite things about my iPhone is that it allows me to snap photos easily in the classroom. It's small enough to fit in my pocket, so I can pull it out and take a quick picture whenever I see something interesting happening. The process is so quick that it has become a natural part of what I do and it doesn't interrupt learning. I love to capture these moments and I love to reflect on them later. This year I noticed that I took lots of pictures during Genius Hour—a period of time each day when students are free to explore and learn about topics of their choice. On a daily basis, there is always a lot going on. A few children might be studying rocks with a magnifying glass, while others are trying to label a diagram with a tool in Pixie. Others are learning about a bird seen during a science observation earlier in the week. Everywhere I look, the room is always filled with a variety of student-led explorations.

When I looked through my latest set of photos from Genius Hour, one group caught my eye. A group of girls interested in rock identification worked for weeks to learn all they could about rocks. Each photo, on its own, merely captured the daily work of this group, but when I looked across several days' photos, I noticed something important. On one day, the girls were poring over a book that explained the different types of rocks. On another day, they were using the class iPod and a rock identification website they had discovered, trying to match their rocks to the names on the site. In other photos, they were using the class iPad to take photos of the rock, drop them into the Explain Everything app, and record conversations about their learning. Some days a notebook sat on one child's lap as she sketched and jotted new ideas about her learning. And on other days, several tools were spread out on the table as the students navigated between rocks and devices.

I thought long and hard about these photos and what they told me about our young readers and writers today. These girls were reading and writing in authentic ways across the course of several days. Each day they used a new tool because it fit their need or purpose at that moment. Each day they grabbed what they needed and didn't seem to give any more thought to choosing an iPad than they did to picking up a crayon. They were not using technology because it was "cool" or because it was the assigned day for a particular tool or app. They were using a particular piece of technology when it made sense for their learning. And they were familiar enough with the tools available to know what they needed. These images pushed my thinking about authenticity in the literacy workshop. *Authenticity is evident when I look around the room and see kids using various tools that meet their needs at the moment.*

When I think about my understanding of authenticity, I remember Lucy Calkins's words. In a Web article titled "Get Real about Reading," she suggests that if we were able to have conversations with great readers,

> I do not think those readers would tell us about making shoe-box dioramas of beloved novels or writing new endings to published stories. They wouldn't talk about sending make-believe letters from one character to another, or about cutting books into sentence strips and reassembling them. Instead, I think that great readers would tell us about weaving reading together with the people and passions of their lives. They would tell us that reading, like writing, is a big thing we do with our whole lives.

Calkins's words have always helped me stay grounded in authenticity in the reading workshop, acknowledging that the work of young readers must be based in the things "real readers" do.

As an elementary teacher, I felt I had this "authenticity thing" under control in my traditional literacy workshop. My students had never spent their workshop time rotating between stations or working through a menu of options. They weren't required to create dioramas or write book reports after they finished books to "prove that they understood" them. Instead, students spent their time in authentic reading experiences, reading real books and responding in authentic ways—

ways that readers outside of school respond. They kept notebooks in which they could track their thinking while they read, they talked to others about what they had read, they shared books that others might enjoy, and they discussed issues that came up in their reading. It was easy for me to use my own reading and writing life to keep myself grounded in authentic literacy practices in the classroom. I could relate to the struggles of my students and connect them to my own experiences, thereby helping the students see that they were not the only ones who sometimes struggled with texts.

But digital tools have complicated all of this. With new possibilities and new tools, my own reading life has changed. I use digital tools in ways that extend, expand, analyze, and record my reading, in ways that make my reading more meaningful. Given my own complex reading habits, I can't merely drop digital tools into the classroom workshop and call that authenticity. I can't ask students to use digital tools in ways that are not authentic to what real readers do. Therefore, I can't assign exercises like creating a Facebook page of a book character—an exercise that feels no more authentic than writing make-believe letters from one character to another.

Our Journey to Understanding Authenticity in a Digital Reading Workshop

One of my biggest lessons about authenticity came from a book trailer project I did several years ago. I wanted to bring digital tools into our literacy work, and I saw book trailers as an "authentic" genre that I could harness to give my third graders an opportunity to show their understanding of their chosen book. I brought all that I knew about genre study to the table, and we examined several of the best book trailers I could find. We studied with a critical eye all of the decisions the creator had to make for a single book trailer. Looking closely at the words spoken, the sound/music, and the visuals of each trailer, students sought to understand the genre and how it could translate to their own creations. I then sent kids off to make their own.

Because I believe in the idea of "teacher as writer," I decided that I too needed to create my own book trailer so that I could understand the process. I settled on a book (*Should I Share My Ice Cream?* by Mo Willems), storyboarded it, and got to work finding images and writing a script. The book trailer was about ice cream, so I decided that ice cream truck music would be a great lead into the video. I spent hours searching for ice cream truck music (which turned out to be more difficult than I anticipated—finding music that both fit my expectations and wasn't bound by copyright), but I eventually discovered sheet music to a song that worked, and I downloaded a piano app onto my iPad. After hours and hours, I couldn't get the sound quite right and finally gave up. I understood frustration, pain, and the feeling of defeat because the sound wasn't what I wanted.

In the midst of a big project, it is easy to get caught up, as I did, in tools. I attempted my book trailer so that I could better understand how some students tinker with elements in their works but never really finish a project. But I also realized that the work I was putting into this book trailer was in no way helping me grow as a reader or writer. I wasn't making any connections or going any deeper with my thinking about the book as I created the book trailer. My focus was on overcoming the technological challenges and the minutia of the work, on meeting the requirements of the assignment. Ultimately, this project was no different from the diorama projects we asked students to do in the eighties; it was just a different medium.

A few years later, one of my fourth-grade students wanted to create a book trailer about a book in a series he had been reading (*The Kingdom Keepers: Disney after Dark* by Ridley Pearson) for our class blog. Ben had watched enough book trailers to know this was something he wanted to try, and he had enough experience with Keynote to know how to go about creating an effective slideshow. We kept a class blog that got a bit of traffic, and he thought the blog audience would like to know about the book. He worked for several days finding the perfect photos, adding the perfect music, and thinking deeply about the book as he created a book trailer he was excited to share with others. This book trailer, the same project I had attempted to assign a few years before, suddenly felt authentic. The process was different because Ben *chose* to do it, his selection of pictures and words helped him to *understand the book in new ways*, and his focus was on his *message and audience* as opposed to trying to integrate technology. Because of each of these aspects of the project, Ben grew as both a reader and a writer and had a different understanding of the book.

Ben's book trailer helped me realize that sometimes creating a book trailer as a response to a book or to share a book with others *is* an authentic experience. As a teacher, however, I can't often justify a whole-class assignment on book trailer creation because the authenticity of that experience would not be the same for all of my students. For most of my students, such an assignment—despite the lure of its technological component—feels too much like "doing school." Ours has been an era in which students have learned to jump through the sometimes meaningless hoops of school, doing things for the sake of school rather than for the love of learning. When that happens, we lose opportunities for authentic learning. In his book *The Game of School*, Robert Fried states,

> It's just that too many of us—students and teachers alike—agree to substitute lesser, symbolic goals for greater and truer ones. When we allow ourselves to gear ourselves up so as to complete school tasks that have little meaning for us aside from the value

of getting them done and over with, we lose touch with our own learning spirit. . . . We become *game players* by reflex and *learners* only on occasion. (14)

Experiences like mine with book trailers have taught the two of us that authenticity in the digital reading workshop is more complex than we realized. Authenticity means that readers:

- do the same reading work in classrooms that they do in the world outside of the classroom;
- have choice in the ways they read and respond to their reading;
- own the reading decisions they make; they are not doing things for the sake of an assignment or project;
- care about the reading work they are doing because it is personal;
- use digital tools as needed based on their purpose; and
- learn digital tools in the midst of learning experiences, not as a separate experience.

Our Lives as Readers Teach Us about Authenticity

Not long ago, we had bad weather in our area. As I tried to figure out where the bad weather was heading, I turned on the TV, popped onto my Twitter account to search my news station's tweets, logged on to Facebook to follow updates by one of our local forecasters, and checked the radar on a weather app on my phone. I did these things simultaneously to get the information I needed. By pulling all of them up at once, I could combine several pieces of information to understand the weather that was coming our way.

This is a big change from the ways we used to get information; only recently have we been able to choose from several sources of information. As readers today, we must have the skills to navigate several types of text. The NCTE policy research brief on reading tells us, "In and out of school, the texts students read vary significantly, from linear text-only books to multimodal textbooks to online hypertexts, each of which places different demands on readers and requires different strategies and approaches to reading" (ix). We've both noticed how our own reading lives have changed because of digital tools. But it is sometimes easy to miss these changes because they have happened slowly over time. It is also easy to assume—erroneously—that our students have these skills and can easily transfer them to school.

We have always known how important it is to bring our own reading lives into the classroom. As we focus more on authentic digital reading, we must continue to ask ourselves questions about our own reading lives so that we can make sure the things we are teaching our students are relevant in and out of school. Some of the questions that have been helpful for us are these:

- What changes have I've noticed in my reading habits over the past several years?
- What am I most surprised about when it comes to the ways my reading has changed?
- What devices do I rely on as a reader?
- Are there certain sites and apps that I visit regularly as a reader?
- How do I respond to my reading?
- Am I part of any social networks specific to readers?
- Do I use any social networks as a way to respond as a reader?
- How have I learned about new digital tools that I use?
- Have I connected with authors or other readers in new ways?
- What are some challenges I face as a reader in this digital age?
- What are the deciding factors for choosing a digital text over a traditional text?
- What types of content do I consider to be "reading"?
- What trends do I see in the reading lives of my friends and colleagues?

Being readers ourselves is the best tool we have to keep our classroom workshops authentic.

In Bill's work as a technology coordinator in schools, he often talks with teachers about modeling in our own practice what we want to see from our students. In one sixth-grade language arts class, he and the teacher had been on a coaching cycle for about three weeks during which they focused their learning on her desire to use technology in a meaningful way with her students. Diana was already a tech-savvy teacher and used a variety of digital tools in her own work, but she was often the only one using technology in her classroom. Whether she was using Google Drive for collaborative planning with her teammates or designing a lesson on her SMART Board, Diana knew the tools and how to use them.

Through many conversations with Bill, Diana determined that she both took her knowledge for granted and expected her students to have more advanced technology skills. She knew that her students had their own personal experiences using some of the very tools she was asking them to use in class, but when they got on the computer at school, they seemed lost. With all of the other demands on Diana's time, integrating technology was often left out of the curriculum because she saw technology as an "extra," something that time just didn't permit. In one particular conversation, she came to see the contradiction between her own use of technology as a teacher and the ease with which she made assumptions about her students' use of technology. Diana needed a plan to create a more authentic means of introducing digital tools in the classroom.

The next week during lunch, Diana brought in a small group of students from her team to talk about what they saw as the struggles of bringing the digital world into schools and what they needed from her to make this integration more effective. "We know how to use the tools," they said, "and if we don't know, we'll figure it out. What we need to know is how to use them in school and what you want us to do with them in class. The computer isn't what gets in our way. It's that we don't know what you want from us. We know how *we* use the tools, but we don't know how *you* use them." Diana quickly learned that she didn't have to teach every single skill for every tool; what she did have to do was explain herself as she was teaching so that students could not only see what she was doing with a specific tool but also know *why* she was doing it.

From this point on, Diana began to talk to her students in a very intentional way about the decisions she was making. She made sure these explanations focused on not just the tools students would be using but also how she used these tools in her everyday practice. She began to make the most of small opportunities. When she did a quick Google search, she talked through why she put quotation marks around the search term, explaining that Google would then give her only results that had that exact term on a given webpage. As she presented with PowerPoint, she stopped for a moment to talk about why she had chosen a specific transition or animation. She brought her inner dialogue into the classroom and let students in on the decisions she made as she used the tools of technology. Within about four weeks, Diana found that some of her students were asking her questions about her own use of technology in and out of the classroom. This opened the door for conversations about ebooks and her own reading life. She shared with them how she used the services of the public library through her tablet so that she could access books and databases without having to actually go to the library. By paying attention to her own literacy, Diana was able to support her students in authentic ways.

We've come to see that authenticity is about more than having students read and write the types of texts they will encounter outside of the classroom. Instead, authenticity is about choice and ownership. If we want our students to be successful digital readers, they need to be able to do more than read a variety of texts. We want them to make good choices about the kinds of texts they select and to respond in ways that make sense for them. If that is our goal, our first step is to make sure we give students opportunities for a variety of reading experiences during reading workshop.

Resources for Authentic Choice in the Reading Workshop

So much of what our students learn is anchored in what we value in the classroom. And often, without even realizing it, our message to students is that we don't value all types of reading and response. We have learned that we need to value all types of reading, to value various types of response, and, most important, to value a student's choice and purpose in reading. One of the ways we do that is by monitoring the types of reading that count in our classrooms.

Just as our own reading lives are changing because of the available texts and tools, our students' reading lives are changing as well. Students today have access to a variety of texts, and the ways in which they access stories and information are expanding. Like us, our students can choose to read a traditional book or an ebook version on their tablets. However, as we have moved to digital workshops, we needed more than a familiarity with just these two platforms. What we and our students were challenged by, especially early on, was finding digital resources that could become a useful part of our workshops. Familiarizing ourselves with several sites and resources helped us expand our knowledge and thus what we valued in our classrooms. Now our students can access news daily on sites like DOGOnews, follow blogs on *Sports Illustrated KIDS*, and read blogs by classmates on Kidblogs. They also can choose to read in ways that combine multiple kinds of texts.

We also found books that expand the ways stories are told. Patrick Carman was one of the first authors who really committed to creating this kind of new reading experience for young readers. Several years ago, Carman authored the Skeleton Creek series, in which the stories are told in different media. The first book in the series starts out as a journal of a boy named Ryan, who is stuck in his room. Throughout the story, Ryan receives video messages from his friend Sarah. Each time this happens, the reader gets the login information to watch Sarah's video, just as Ryan would. The text and the video work seamlessly together to tell one story. Neither stands alone.

Other books such as *The Search for WondLa* (DiTerlizzi) do similar things by combining digital tools with a more traditional text. *Chopsticks* by Jessica Anthony and Rodrigo Corral is a book told in many pieces. The book was created simultaneously in paper format and as an interactive iPad app, and the reader puts pieces of a girl's story together from page one. *The Fantastic Flying Books of Mr. Morris Lessmore* (Joyce and Bluhm) was created as an interactive ebook that draws the reader into a powerful story.

In addition, we are always on the lookout for websites that are appropriate for readers in grades 3–8. Many sites such as PebbleGo, Wonderopolis, and DOGOnews provide our students with daily online content. The reading possibilities are broad, and if we are to keep literacy authentic, we must value all of these texts in our classrooms.

Third-grade teacher Bev Gallagher is adept at exploring ways to authentically embed digital tools and resources in her curriculum. In the following classroom vignette, Bev shares the ways she expanded her culminating poetry project to use digital tools.

Voices from the Classroom

Integrating Technology and Poetry

Bev Gallagher
Grade 3 Teacher
Princeton Day School
Princeton, New Jersey

One of the wonders of teaching third grade is immersing students in poetry all year long. Whether it is the monthly poetry extravaganza highlighting a specific poet or using poetry to springboard a unit, the results of poetry immersion can be profound and compelling. By April students are engaged in compiling an anthology. After reading many poetry books and appreciating the craft of poets, students slowly begin to take on the role of anthologist, carefully choosing and sorting through volumes as well as their own writing folders to craft an anthology with their own stamp. Over the years, my colleagues and I have begun to see where technology plays a role and how we can weave it into the curriculum deliberately and thoroughly.

This year we made a number of changes to the students' rubrics. All of the students maintain blogs, and the teaching team wanted the kids to post at least two entries detailing their experience of creating a poetry anthology. How we loved reading about a new poet they discovered, a poem that touched them, and the entries about pantoums or reversos—forms of poems that the students loved and emulated. We also had them read other poets' blogs. Sylvia Vardell (http://poetryforchildren.blogspot.com/) has a wonderful site listing many great poets. We had students choose two to read and add commentary.

In past years, we talked about the role of an anthologist and looked carefully at several anthologists' work, eager to discover how they created their books. This year we thought a Skype visit would be a great addition to the project. A number of poet friends said they would love to try a session with the third graders, so we turned to poet extraordinaire Nikki Grimes (www.nikkigrimes.com) for her counsel. What an amazing session. Students knew her work and now they could ask the hard questions: How did she decide on the poems to include in her collection *Hopscotch Love*? How did she find writing a poem for the collection *Lives*, edited by Lee Bennett Hopkins? This live conversation was incredible, and for thirty minutes we were eagerly asking questions and discussing answers.

As the students and I decided on the final form for their anthologies, we took the final bend in the road. We really wanted to create ebook collections that students could mail to their family members and friends. After looking at a number of possibilities for creating ebooks, students ultimately wrote beautiful introductions and used Tellagami (https://tellagami.com/), a mobile app that allows users to write a script and create animated videos of their stories. The kids adored using this app, and it was a perfect way to introduce their anthologies and draw readers into their books. They were able to record a favorite poem on the classroom iPads and have readers click to hear their voices. Finally, the whole project was housed on Book Creator (www.redjumper.net/bookcreator).

One of the great benefits of transforming the project from traditional to digital text was working closely with the technology teacher. We discovered that technology is best woven into the classroom when it feels meaningful and follows the structure of reading and writing workshop. Not only were students able to access some of the poetry books online for reading, but they were also able to preview new ones to add to our library. The opportunity to Skype with a poet was an immense treat, one that would have been hard to duplicate in any other fashion. And creating an ebook is a transferable skill, one they will put to good use the following year.

When technology is used in a way that authentically enhances the work of the classroom, the students achieve and acquire another layer of learning—and enjoy the experience and process more deeply.

Another colleague, seventh-grade language arts teacher Cryslynn Billingsley, shares the ways she worked to embed digital tools into her workshop in an authentic fashion, even though she did not see herself as a "tech person."

Voices from the Classroom

Bringing in the World

Cryslynn Billingsley
Grade 7 English Language Arts Teacher
Parkway Northeast Middle School
Creve Coeur, Missouri

Last fall I was preparing a lesson for my seventh-grade English language arts class about the right to an education. Students were to take part in a literature discussion. They would also be asked to write an argument piece on the following prompt: What is your position on the right to an education? I wanted students to form their own opinions about educational systems around the world and to examine what education looks like internationally, nationally, and locally. What are the similarities, differences, and problems in the educational systems? Why the ambiguities in the different systems? Who decides who gets educated? What are some solutions to the problems in the systems? This topic was a complex one for students, so I needed to figure out how to give them more background experience with the topic. I needed them to "see" some things about education if I wanted them to discuss and write about it, and they needed time to access the information about education around the world in a variety of ways. This project needed to mean something to them—and yes, of course, to engage them. This is where digital literacy and technology came in very handy.

I was able to offer students a variety of texts to hook their attention and keep this complex topic relevant to them. I showed them a video clip about a student from another country who came to America to attend school—there were no schools in her village. We read an infographic map that showed statistics about education from all around the world, and we coded it by putting a checkmark by the information we already knew and a question mark by facts we were still curious about. We watched the TED talk "Dare to Educate Afghan Girls" by Shabana Basij-Rasikh and a report from NBC News explaining how the United States lags in student achievement and how many students drop out per day in this country. We listened to an audio clip of a mom calling into a radio station to ask questions about the gender gap. We read an article that explained what the achievement gap is and who it affects and why. The last thing students saw in preparation for the discussion was coverage on Fox 2 News about student transfers to other districts after their neighborhood districts lost accreditation. As each piece of information was shown, played, or provided to students, the anticipation built—they were ready to make a claim about their stance on the right to an education. Students could return to any of the clips, articles, and audio because I put the links on my website. With the use of technology, I was able to provide students with a lot of background information and experience on a complex topic. Every single student had an entry point into the discussion and the writing on the topic. This process also demonstrated how to curate information from the Web for a specific purpose.

After teaching this lesson, I sent the following email to a few colleagues about the journey I've had with technology:

> I have been teaching myself how to utilize Edline, Google apps, and other Web tools for lessons in ELA. (I love Edline, by the way!) I was thinking about how I thought I was not a "technology person" when now I see that my classroom would not survive without it. Even when I use a Web tool for something in class, whether it be something brief or extended, my students show understanding in ways I had not imagined. I thought being a technology person meant knowing everything about it, but what I have realized is that teaching 21st century learners is a learning process for teachers and a process for students in learning the various ways technology can be used in life—even academically!

The next morning, I got a notification from my Twitter feed with this message:

Kevin Beckner @KevinBeckner · Dec 11

7th grade ELA Teacher: "Teaching 21st Century learners is a learning process for teachers..." @Ccblivelife (1/2)

↩   ⇄ 1   ★ 1   •••

Kevin Beckner @KevinBeckner · Dec 11

It's also " a process for students in learning the various ways technology can be used in life- even academically!" @Ccblivelife (2/2)

↩   ⇄ 1   ★   •••

This is what digital literacy does—it keeps us connected. My colleague was not in my classroom for the lesson, but I shared it with him and he shared it with others. How else could I bring the realities of education around the world to my students? I was able to offer them information about systems from around the world in ways they typically access information. Students are always watching videos about all kinds of things—why not for my ELA class? Students listen to the radio and podcasts too. Because students read for different reasons, I had them read and code a few articles and infographics on the topic we were studying. They interacted with the topic through technology, engaging in a dialogue about educational systems around the world all while sitting in my classroom. I interacted with my colleagues about what I learned, and they shared that learning with others too.

My students are twenty-first-century learners who consume information in so many ways. Developing this lesson, I realized that I am a real technology teacher because I have become intentional about the ways student learning is facilitated in my classroom. Maybe I'm not perfect at every tech tool I use and introduce, but I am open to the process of learning in order to meet the needs of all my students. I meet my students where their thinking exists and thrives. I must continue to model the use of critical technology skills and competencies required for success in today's society. And I will continue to seek out ways to facilitate learning through digital literacy and technology.

Not only are the formats of the texts we are reading changing, but so too are the ways in which readers can respond to their reading. Social networks such as Goodreads and Shelfari allow readers to log and share reading with their online networks. Twitter and Facebook allow readers, authors, and publishers to communicate regularly. While readers have always responded in various ways to and about their reading, the possibilities for how they can share their thinking and with whom they can communicate are expanding rapidly. Because students have opportunities to share their responses to reading beyond their teachers, reader response has become authentic. So much of what we know about reader response transfers to the digital world readers now live in. As Louise Rosenblatt taught us, "The reader brings to the work personality traits, memories of past events, present needs and preoccupations, a particular mood of the moment and a particular physical condition. These and many other elements in a never-to-be-duplicated combination determine his response to the text" (31). Digital tools and social media have opened up new ways for our students to respond personally and thoughtfully as readers.

Creating Authentic Experiences with Multiple Tools

Just as students in a traditional reading workshop might be reading different books, students in a digital reading workshop are probably reading on different devices and using different tools to make sense of their reading. Whether it's Popplet or another tool, teachers have to consider how these tools fit into the bigger picture of a student's learning life. Over the last few years, many school districts have given students permission to bring their own devices to school for use in the classroom. These Bring Your Own Device (BYOD) initiatives were typically started as a way to supplement the existing technology in schools because it was too expensive to buy every student a device. By allowing students to connect to the district network, schools didn't limit students to a computer provided by the school, thus saving the district money.

My (Franki's) district began a BYOD program recently, and many of my third graders began bringing devices to school on a daily basis. I found that the BYOD policy challenged me to think differently about what I expected from students. I quickly realized how much control I had to let go of in order to use these devices, but I was amazed at how many possibilities opened up when I let go. The learning curve was steep, though: I came to see that I had to think differently about tools when different students had different tools at their fingertips. I had been unaware of how much my teaching focused on a single tool rather than on the learning or thinking I wanted students to do. Focusing on the learning rather than the tool created a more authentic workshop and at the same time freed me up to concentrate on the learning and worry less about the tool. And when we added five to six BYOD devices to the three iPads and four laptops already in the room, the variety of choices became more apparent to students.

Several things changed almost immediately when students brought their devices from home:

- During independent reading time, some students read paper books and articles while others read a Web-based piece on their iPod.
- In book clubs on *The Quirks: Welcome to Normal?*, some students had a paper copy of the book while others had an ebook version. Some students got ready for the book club meetings by adding sticky notes or jotting down thoughts in a notebook, while others used the annotation tool on their Kindle.
- In read-aloud, some students continued to write in their reading notebook while others began to use their iPad to track thinking in Notability or on Popplet.
- As a response to reading, some students created a blog post to tell others about a book while another told a friend about the book in face-to-face conversation.

Shared Experiences to Support Authentic Choices

One of the core structures of reading workshop is share sessions and response. In traditional reading workshops, this might mean gathering in the meeting area at the end of each workshop to share great books, new strategies, and things we learned about ourselves as readers. As we move to a digital environment, we have opened our teaching to the multiple tools that can help us share all of these things. We want our students to have lots of possibilities, so we use our own experiences as readers to introduce various ways to read and respond to text. Because we believe that authenticity is grounded in purposeful choice, our students must know what is possible, and we have found shared experiences are powerful ways to focus on thinking while exposing students to a new tool. As Ruth Ayres and Christi Overman tell us in *Celebrating Writers*, "One of the best places to learn the nuances of social media is in school, but it is only possible if teachers establish an online presence as a classroom" (40). We have the opportunity and responsibility in classrooms to help students use tools authentically and to share their thinking with various audiences.

In our workshops, we have tried to embed tools into our routines that stretch thinking and give readers new opportunities for understanding. By using these collaboratively first, students can then choose to use them independently when the tools seem right for their purposes. Some of our favorite tools are described in Figure 3.1.

Learning Digital Tools Authentically

My (Franki's) principal popped into my room this fall asking me to give her a five-minute lesson on Evernote. She had downloaded the Evernote app to her iPad because she knew many of her teachers were using it to collect student assessment

---

Figure 3.1. A sampling of the authors' favorite online tools for classroom use.

Padlet is a digital bulletin board that allows users to add sticky notes as well as photos, links, videos, and more. As a shared experience, Padlet is a great tool for collecting thinking and connecting pieces during a class read-aloud or a book club discussion. Students can add items in real time, or the board can be used to collect things in a more formal way. When we read aloud *The One and Only Ivan* (Applegate), we used Padlet to collect resources connected with the book. When we began the book, the board included the author's website, a video about Ivan, and a link to a book trailer, and we added from there.

Corkulous is another digital bulletin board tool; it allows users to add sticky notes and organize them by color, label, and so forth. Franki recently used Corkulous as a shared experience with her third graders. During their read-aloud of Barbara O'Connor's *How to Steal a Dog*, instead of charting thinking on chart paper, students recorded their thoughts and discussions on a Corkulous board as it was projected on a screen. Throughout the read-aloud, students could refer to past thinking, add new thinking, reorganize thinking, and change thinking. Although the main goals of the tool are similar to those when using chart paper (to track thinking while reading in order to better understand a book), Corkulous gave the readers more options for organizing and reorganizing information, so the conversation was richer because of the tool.

Popplet is a tool that allows users to track and organize thinking in a Web-type format. Users can add text, images, and more to each thought. The thoughts can then be connected in various ways using the connector tool. Organizing thinking by changing the color of the box, the color of the text, and the way it connects to other thoughts makes Popplet a great tool for pushing thinking and understanding. Recently, one of Franki's third graders used this tool to annotate thinking during her reading of *A Snicker of Magic* (Lloyd). She jotted down her thoughts as she read just as she might have done on sticky notes. But Popplet allowed her to color-code her responses to reflect on the kinds of thinking she was doing and which type helped her better understand the text.

Wordle allows users to synthesize thinking in a word cloud. By adding lists of words, this tool creates a word cloud that gives more weight to words used more often than others. This visual representation is a powerful one. Recently, Franki used Wordle with her fourth graders to synthesize their thinking around a read-aloud. After finishing about half of the book *Wonder* (Palacio), each student thought of one word to describe the character. Collecting those words on Wordle gave us a great deal to build on in future conversations around the book.

Google Forms provides a different way to keep a reading log. Instead of keeping a paper log, students can fill out a Google Form with information such as title, author, and genre to track their reading over time.

Goodreads is a social networking site for readers. Having a classroom Goodreads account allows students under the age of thirteen to experience the power of an online reading community. A classroom account allows students to rate and review books, get recommendations, and read others' thoughts on books.

Blogs are another way for students to respond to books with an authentic audience. Students can blog individually in a closed classroom setting, or they can share their reading with the world on a class blog.

A class **Twitter** account is a great way to respond to reading. Tweeting about books read, thoughts on reading, and messages to authors opens up possibilities for more global conversations around books.

---

data and for kidwatching. With her cursory knowledge of the possibilities, she thought it would be the perfect tool for the classroom observation portion of our new teacher evaluation system. In a few minutes, my colleague and I taught her the basics of creating notes in Evernote and answered a few of her questions about taking pictures right in the app. Having mastered the basics, she was off. That very day our principal began using Evernote when she was in classrooms, and she eventually taught herself the things she needed to know as she needed them. She had a basic understanding of the tool's purpose, got a quick tutorial on the pieces she needed right away, and then continued to learn in the context of using Evernote for authentic purposes. As we talked about her experiences later, I couldn't help but remember all of the professional development on technology I have attended over the years where I learned everything there was to know about a tool or program. As I walked into those sessions, I was typically excited to learn a new tool and really dive into how to use it, but I usually left feeling overwhelmed, not knowing where to begin. I realized that we need to be authentic not only with our literacy practices but also about how we embed tools in our classrooms. Just as we don't learn a tool all at once, neither do our students. Learning the capabilities of tools while using them in authentic ways makes the most sense for all of us. Those are the experiences that tend to stick with us. We don't need to know the minute details of every program we run across. We need to know enough to get us going, and we learn what we need as we need it.

In her fourth-grade classroom, Ann Marie Corgill embedded this quick technology learning into her daily morning meeting time.

Voices from the Classroom

Technology Tips and Techniques

Ann Marie Corgill
Grade 4 Teacher
Cherokee Bend Elementary School
Mountain Brook, Alabama

One of the ways I like to set kids up for success and engagement in reading digital texts is through a routine I created for my fourth graders called "Technology Tips and Techniques." When I first implemented this routine, as soon as school started, I began introducing interesting apps, websites, and technology tools in our Morning Meeting time.

My goal in creating this valuable routine in our classroom was to give children multiple opportunities to read, explore, and use these sites and apps in our literacy workshops throughout the day to build their repertoire as readers and savvy users of technology. Several times a week, at the end of Morning Meeting, I shared something "techy and new." Eyes brightened, heads turned, and there was an excitement I hadn't seen, especially with the children who hadn't yet learned to love reading.

For example, at the beginning of our nonfiction unit of study, I shared Wonderopolis with the kids. Wonderopolis is a site designed to ignite curiosity and imagination that might then lead to discovery and in-depth learning about a particular topic. The room filled with productive chatter and questions as soon as the page opened. The children were so intrigued that we also signed up for the "Wonder of the Day," a daily email message about a particular Wonder. Children not only had opportunities to read and explore the information on the site, but they also looked forward to reading and then discussing the daily Wonder sent directly to our class account.

As the year progressed, students took over this section of the Morning Meeting and shared tools and tips they had discovered while working independently in the workshop.

I started with one goal—to ignite a curiosity in my class of readers and digital natives—but as the year progressed, Technology Tips and Techniques became much more than I ever expected. This seemingly simple and short morning routing became an integral part of the children's growth as readers, writers, and communicators—of both traditional and digital texts.

Keeping in mind this notion of authentic embedding of technology, we have learned to plan in ways that keep us focused on the literacy rather than the tools. Instead of deciding to do a two-week study of how to read on the Web or to blog throughout the year or to read the daily Wonder on Wonderopolis, we build options into the day so that students can be purposeful about the things they want to read and the ways in which they read them. We make sure we are embedding digital texts throughout the literacy workshop and throughout the day. If our students are to make purposeful decisions as readers and writers, we have to ensure they have lots of experiences with a variety of print and digital texts for a variety of purposes.

Instead of creating lessons specifically on tool or craft, then, we try to see the connections and the ways the tools and the content work together to give readers a message and help kids to become more effective readers. As we've stated multiple times, readers and writers make so many decisions on a daily basis that focusing on a specific tool isn't an effective way to foster independent thinking and habits.

Students need many skills as they consume and produce texts. We've realized that although it is often easier to create lessons around individual technology—i.e., to develop specific "skills" in isolation—it is more powerful if all of the literacy work is integrated with the tool that matches it best. For example, instead of holding a mini-lesson on how to add a photo to a blog post, we might instead work on a shared blog post together, choose an image that would enhance the piece, and then add it as part of the shared writing. When studying a genre, we are careful to use books as well as videos. Instead of a lesson on tagging, each shared post we write might include a conversation about tags that might work and how they can help us organize information. Each reading we share after that includes a conversation about how we might or might not use the tags to learn more and be more effective readers.

My (Franki's) students now learn specific tools in a more integrated way than they did a few years ago. In the past, I thought about literacy skills and technology skills as very different. I'd spend time on a mini-lesson about writing a good nonfiction lead, and later we might have a mini-lesson on navigating a website. Although these two mini-lessons are still valuable, our shared experiences integrate the literacy and the technology more often, making it a seamless experience for kids. With this change in my instruction, my students now use tools easily because we've used them together as a class. Other changes to our classroom work that integrate tools into our workshop include the following:

- We are careful about navigating between chart paper and a digital tool when modeling. If we are creating a table in science, we might draw one on chart paper one week and then open up Apple's Pages app to create a chart the next time. Just as we don't stop to verbalize what we are doing on chart paper, we don't verbalize it with Pages. But when students see us using both, they learn that sometimes it's best to grab a marker and sometimes it's better to grab a laptop.

- Although conferring doesn't often focus on a tool, a tool might come into play when a child is struggling with an aspect of reading. If a digital bulletin board seems like a better fit for annotating thinking than a notebook, a conference is a great place to introduce the idea and the tool simultaneously.

- Student experts often take time in workshop to sit next to a child using a new tool. Experts emerge quickly and they are often the people who run a quick mini-session or meet with a student during workshop time.

- Playing with and exploring new tools is important. Genius Hour, a time each week when students are empowered to explore their own passions and interests, and indoor recess give students time for discovery.

Focusing on authenticity requires us to think about a reader's choice and ownership of a text, how the reader responds to the text, and how the text relates to the tools for reading.

Teachers have strived for years to provide kids with authentic classroom experiences, and the rationale behind this stance hasn't changed as we move toward a digital environment. We still seek to create relevant and meaningful ways to give kids opportunities to work with all kinds of text so that multiple platforms and approaches to reading become integrated into their daily lives. Authenticity is what connects the work of school to the work of being a reader, helping students learn to embrace their reading lives.

Striving for authenticity in the literacy workshop should be a goal for all reading teachers. In the next chapter, we discuss the importance of making intentional decisions about the tools, content, and classroom strategies that will help set the groundwork for the authentic experiences we want for kids.

Chapter Four

What Really Matters?
Becoming Intentional
Decision Makers

A s we get out of the car and head into the library, ten-year-old Molly grabs my (Bill's) hand and gives it an impatient tug. "Hurry!" she says. "There's a book waiting for me." Picking up the pace as requested, I ask her what she has on hold. "*The Trolley to Yesterday* by John Bellairs," she replies. "It's been out at school for the last month and I couldn't wait anymore. It's finally here! Let's go, let's go!" As we make our way to the holds shelves, Molly finds her book and takes a moment to peruse what other people are reading. "It's good that all these people have found their just-right books," she says quietly to herself before heading off to take a look at what else she might want to take home today.

Going to the library with Molly and her brother, Maxwell, is always an adventure. They are both strong readers. They know what they like, but they are open to suggestions and are willing to take a chance on a book if something about it strikes them. Their approach to choosing a book is a direct result of their experiences in the classroom. From kindergarten through fourth grade, they have been immersed in a culture of reading in which they discuss, review, and work with books in authentic ways. They also seek out authors whose books they've read and liked or series that they've heard their teacher talk about, and they almost always read the description on the back cover. They know that they make decisions as they read and that these decisions impact their understanding and enjoyment of the book.

As intentional as Molly and Maxwell are about choosing traditional books, they are equally intentional when consuming digital content. In the fall of 2013, Molly and Maxwell spent hours poring over rubber band bracelet videos on You-Tube looking for new charms and projects they could create and share with their friends. Molly was critical in her assessment of the videos and moved quickly from one to another. She knew what she needed to learn in order to start a new project. She looked for common features of the videos but also went far beyond the actual content and the making of the project to analyze the videos themselves in order to choose the ones that would be most useful to her.

One day I overheard Molly talking to her brother. "See this one," she said, "it has a title before it starts. It's more professional; she must know what she's talking about. This one doesn't," she says pointing at another suggested video, "and look, it's fifteen minutes long. There's no way I'm watching that when they didn't take the time to make a title slide. They probably did the whole thing on screen without editing anything out. It will probably be hard to follow."

Without direction, Molly had watched enough videos to discern what was going to be worth her time. She had noticed patterns in the videos and made her own conclusions about what was valuable and what wasn't. She especially liked the *Made by Mommy* videos (www.youtube.com/user/mbmcrafts) because they went step by step, used graphics and diagrams, and included a supplies list that told her what she needed before she got started. As a reader, Molly knew how to navigate these YouTube videos in a very intentional way. As Franki and I watch the young readers in our classrooms and schools, we continue to be struck by the ways in which they—like Molly and Maxwell—transfer skills back and forth between digital and print texts to make sense of their reading.

This Is Not an Either/Or Conversation

As we wrote this book, we began to look more closely at the decisions we make as teachers and to analyze why we make those decisions. We knew that we both were heavy digital readers and we felt confident in moving between mediums, but we hadn't studied our digital reading habits closely or compared them to the more traditional habits ingrained in our reading lives.

We both still buy lots of traditional books and magazines in paper form but, not surprisingly, much of our reading is also done on electronic devices. To a great extent, the platform we choose depends on the type of reading we are doing and what will be most convenient for our purpose. These are conscious choices we make as readers because of the way our reading has changed over time. Every choice we make as readers is an intentional one. We are intentional not only about *what* we choose to read, but also about *how* we choose to read it. We are intentional when we choose a paper copy of a book over the electronic version. We are intentional about taking a break from reading a print review to hop on the Internet to check out other reviews. We are intentional when we send a quick email to a friend in the midst of our reading to ask if they've read the article and seek their opinion about it, and we are intentional when we decide that something we're reading is worth sharing on Twitter or Facebook.

One of these moments of intentionality came for me (Bill) as I was starting a grad class last fall. For the first time in my coursework, I was given the opportunity to use a digital textbook. I ended up buying access to the book for six months on Google Books, and off I went. Even though I have been reading on digital devices for years, I found this to be an interesting experiment because it was the first digital text I was assigned. I quickly discovered that many of the reading habits I'd used with more traditional textbooks got in my way. At times I longed to be able to flip back and forth between sections of the book to examine diagrams or reread various passages. But I quickly figured out the meaning-making and annotation strategies I would use to understand this academic text and found that it was much different from reading for leisure or even professional books. I still highlighted the text I wanted to remember, made notes in the margins, and bookmarked pages I knew I would want to refer to later. What differed was that this time I felt as if more was at stake. I was in a class where I would be given a grade and be held responsible for the material. Although I relied on the reading skills I had honed in the pages of print books, my options had just expanded. I liberally used the search function to connect ideas and often looked for further explanation of the book's concepts in Google Scholar and other databases, and I took external notes and made lists in Evernote. The tools I relied on daily melded with my academic reading needs, and I could move seamlessly between the two. This experience allowed me to examine the way that I use text and to be self-aware enough to understand the strategies I might need to employ as I made meaning of this text.

There is plenty to be learned by watching kids as they use various types of digital texts. So often they are far more astute at recognizing what they are doing than we give them credit for. They may not initially make the connection between their own reading habits and the strategies they employ because, like us, they take their ability to move between digital and traditional texts for granted. That being said, the more self-aware we are about the choices we make and the more we recognize how intentional we are in these decisions, the better we can use the tools and strategies available to us and the better we can understand the texts we read.

Outside of school, our students are growing up with many more choices as readers and writers, and part of our job as teachers is to help them be intentional in their choices. As tech-savvy adult readers, we know that becoming a digital reader is not an either/or conversation. We know that it doesn't necessarily mean giving up more traditional reading habits. We know that for our students, being digital readers means being able to navigate intentionally between print and digital resources.

Whether we are teaching students how to be intentional about what they read or about the strategies they use to make sense of a text, intentionality is especially essential when it comes to digital reading. Intentionality is the difference between thoughtful understanding and random clicking and scanning. We know that contemporary readers are adept at reading both digital and traditional texts—which is what we want for our students. But we can't wait until they are successful readers of traditional texts before we support them in becoming digital readers. These skills must be integrated into all kinds of reading throughout the day.

What Do Intentional Readers Do?

Every time a student picks up a book or logs on and becomes a reader, he or she is making choices about how to interact with content. Again, the NCTE policy research brief on reading highlights the complexity of literacy today: "In and out of school, the texts students read vary significantly, from linear text-only books to multimodal textbooks to online hypertexts, each of which places different demands on readers and requires different strategies and approaches to reading" (ix). Learning to make purposeful decisions is more important than ever. If we want students to be intentional users of digital tools, we need to focus on the how and why of using digital tools for student learning and to build on what they already do outside of school. Our students may be comfortable on computers, but that doesn't necessarily mean they have the skills to do all that is needed to meet the goals we have for them as digital readers. If they do not learn to be intentional decision makers, they might spend year after year merely clicking and skimming for facts. As Angela Maiers reminds us in her post "Tech Comfy NOT Tech Savvy!," "Being tech-comfy . . . does not guarantee [readers'] proficiencies automatically grow into new and sophisticated literacies or online competencies as info-sumers, critical thinkers, and savvy participants in a digital space." Students need us to help them navigate the strategies and habits needed to become literate in these areas, but we've found that our students are definitely up for the challenge. While tech-comfiness alone is not enough, as Dahlia Hamza Constantine, a participant in an online course offered by Choice Literacy, recently commented on the course wiki, "Their tech-comfiness allows them to dig in fearlessly and learn quickly."

Whether students are immersed in traditional or in digital texts, we must help them learn to be strategic and intentional about the ways they interact with them. Being intentional means that readers:

- Have strategies for choosing texts
- Know when to reread
- Know when to live with confusion
- Have purpose for their reading
- Know their own strengths and weaknesses as readers
- Know how to stick with something hard
- Use strategies flexibly to build deep understanding
- Move between formats and devices fluently

We agree with Laura Sessions Stepp when she says, "For a child to learn what he loves to do, he first has to find out what is possible. He must be exposed to new places, people and ideas and encouraged to try new activities he has never tried; to hone newfound skills" (28). But possibilities are only the first step to intentionality. Yes, as teachers we have to ensure that our students know what is possible as readers, writers, and learners. But then we have to give them opportunities to use what they know to make intentional choices. And we have to teach them the tools and strategies to make purposeful decisions. Keeping our eye on literacy while embedding the tools naturally in the curriculum seems to be the most critical component in our students' learning.

The Teacher's Role: Scaffolding Intentionality by Text Choice

One of the most obvious ways we can teach students to be intentional is through the text selections we make as teachers. As with any text, scaffolding is critical. If our students constantly read digital content that is too hard for them, they can never be intentional because they are always struggling. If they are always reading content that is too easy, there is no need to make decisions as a reader. We know this to be true of the traditional texts in our classroom library as well as the texts that we introduce to students in order to meet our curricular goals and help them continue to improve as readers. This is also true of the media we link to on our classroom websites. The decisions we make about the texts our students have access to directly influence the work students do as they respond to texts and create their own.

Over the years, in our own lives and as we've watched our students, we have seen a huge growth in the types of digital texts available. If we want our students to be purposeful and intentional about their use of digital tools, we have to think carefully about the tools and sites they will access when they are in our classrooms. For students to make purposeful decisions, they need a variety of options. If everyone reads the same article or visits the same website each day, if we tell students which links are important or conduct all the searches, student intentionality is limited and we are doing the work for them.

Our responsibility is to show our students what is possible with online reading. Just as we fill our classrooms with great children's literature, we must also fill our classrooms with great online resources for our students to read and explore. We are careful to read widely and to find quality books with captivating characters to share with our students. We are picky about the books we bring into our classroom libraries, so we must be picky about the sites and tools we introduce to our students. Every link we share on the homepage of our classroom webpage and every site we ask students to visit during class time or for homework gives our students and their families information about what it means to be literate in today's world.

Jillian Heise shares the thought process she went through to include the most pertinent and useful digital texts in her multigenre unit.

Voices from the Classroom

Reading Multigenre Text: Finding Inspiration Online

Jillian Heise
Grade 7/8 Language Arts Teacher
Indian Community School of Milwaukee
Franklin, Wisconsin

Whether I'm in the classroom or at home outside of the school day, my teacher mind is constantly assessing everything I see and read for its inherent value, but also for its possible classroom applications. Much of the media I take in each day is from online sources: Twitter, Facebook, blogs, videos, news outlets, magazines, journals, etc. The reality is that the media many of my students are consuming outside of school are digital also, so it's important that I bring my experience and mindset into the classroom and teach my students how to become more critical consumers of that information. Thus, I'm always on the lookout for digital text that I can bring in to share with them and use in lessons.

One day I was perusing my Twitter feed from my couch at home after school, and an image in a tweet caught my eye that immediately made me think of my students. It was a striking image of a Native American elder standing in a field with turquoise necklaces cascading down her neck. It was a positive and modern image of who Native Americans are today. Since 100 percent of my students are from Native tribes, I pay attention when I find cultural representations that I might be able to bring to their attention. This image led me to start clicking through links and online searches to discover where it was from, and that's how I discovered Matika Wilbur and her Project 562, which became the inspiration for a multigenre digital reading experience for my students. I knew it would be engaging for my students because it would relate to them personally, and it would also portray their cultures in a positive light and touch on topics of importance to their perceptions and futures.

I envisioned implementing this project in my classroom in a way that would lead to opportunities for students to engage in a bit of digital reading, viewing, and inquiry as they took inspiration from the original project to culminate in their own version. I knew it could also tie into the unit on narrative writing we were engaged in at the time—but instead of their own narratives, students would be sharing someone else's story. They would have the chance to learn and share tribal members' stories of being Native in contemporary society. Although I could easily have printed out some materials and read them with my students, I wanted students to take ownership of this project, and since I knew many resources were available online, I set the kids free to inquire on their own, allowing them to develop a deeper understanding of the project, have a more personalized experience, and have multiple chances and ways to engage in digital reading.

Before setting my students loose to follow their inquiries, I wanted to ensure that they had an understanding of the big picture, so I provided a brief overview of how I had discovered this project and then introduced the variety of digital reading opportunities available to them: the Project 562 blog, two Kickstarter campaign pages that funded the project, videos from both campaigns in which Matika Wilbur explains the project goals and progress, and four different news articles about Matika and Project 562. My students were anxious to get started, and immediately I heard mouse clicks, typing keys, and conversation about what students were finding online. They were learning about the purpose of the project and also engaging in some critical reading as they determined whether the articles were positively and accurately representing Project 562. I could see the focus in my students' actions as they clicked through screens and skimmed articles to decide which ones to read, and when it came time to give the warning to log off computers, there were audible groans in the room and requests to "do it again tomorrow." I had a surprise lined up for tomorrow, though, when my students would be engaging in another form of digital reading: watching Matika Wilbur's TEDx talk titled "Surviving Disappearance, Re-Imagining and Humanizing Native Peoples." Showing this video gave my students another opportunity to engage in critical thinking through digital reading of visual text, but beyond that, bringing a "speaker" into our classroom led to more engagement and buy-in on the entire project. My students now talk as if they are on a first name basis with Matika, and through the use of her videos in the classroom, in a sense they feel they know her.

After reading multiple digital sources, my students had a better understanding of the goals of our project inspired by Project 562. We named our version ICS Project 12, referring to the twelve tribes represented by the students at our school. As my students started brainstorming questions to ask, determining who they wanted to profile for their piece, conducting interviews, and writing and revising the narratives they crafted to share the stories of Native people today, they demonstrated that the digital reading they had done at the start of the project gave them a deeper understanding of the topic than they would have had if I had simply told them about it.

As I created this project plan, guided my students through it, worked with them on their writing, and watched them present their pieces to the school, it was apparent that starting the project with digital text had been the right choice. References to "text" in educational standards are common, but nothing in them says that text has to be print. In our technology-centric world, more and more of the texts that people encounter every day are not only digital but also sometimes primarily visual. Photos, videos, speeches, and articles are all texts in my classroom, and these multigenre texts offer unique opportunities for my students to practice reflecting on and critically analyzing what they take in from what they read or watch. This project started digitally from the moment inspiration struck and continued to be digital as my students learned about and researched the topic. All of this digital reading led to a project that I hadn't planned to do this year but that became a highlight because of its meaningfulness and power for my students and the school community.

Jillian Heise's students are learning what is possible with digital tools; once they know what is possible, they can begin to make connections to their own lives outside of school. To ensure our students have a variety of thoughtful and meaningful experiences with the digital tools available to them in the classroom, reflective questions keep us focused on the goals we have for our students and help us use our time with them wisely:

- How do the sites and apps that we share with students help them to become better readers and writers?
- Have we made sure students have enough choice in their reading and writing?
- Do the sites and apps we introduce to students dictate how they engage with a text, or do readers have choices to make?
- Is the site set up in a way that invites readers to make decisions about how to navigate?
- What digital opportunities or invitations do we give to our students in both structured (in-class work) and independent (homework) work?
- How are learning tasks assigned? Are most assignments pencil and paper, or are digital tools part of the expectation?
- Are all students expected to do the same tasks on digital tools, or are they given choices in how to complete their assignments?

These questions help us stay honest about how much we are really embedding digital tools and texts into every child's day. They help us think about where we are relying solely on traditional texts and where we are limiting the variety of texts students encounter. Through this reflection, we can think more deeply about our students' needs and the reading opportunities we encourage so that they can gain experience with a variety of tools and content and become independent decision makers.

Figure 4.1 shares some of the sites we make available to our students to support their intentional choices. We have been curating this list from the many sites available and recognize that, while it's not all-inclusive, it provides entry points for a wide variety of students. We like these sites because each one gives students great content and information but also offers readers different choices to make in order to better understand what they are reading. Individually, each provides great opportunities for growth in digital reading. But together they do much more than that. Collectively, these sites provide options that encourage young readers to develop digital reading skills.

Figure 4.1. Websites useful for supporting students' intentional choices.

Website	Description	Ways It Supports Students in Making Intentional Choices as Readers
PebbleGo www.pebblego.com	This subscription site is designed for students in grades K–3 but is perfect for older elementary students who are just learning to navigate online nonfiction. There is a good variety of media, and support for text and vocabulary are embedded.	• Text can be read to students. • Good mix of visuals and text. • Sound features. • Video features. • Layout supports young students in learning to navigate content.
National Geographic Kids http://kids.nationalgeographic.com	Includes a variety of text types that help students learn about locations, animals, and science.	• Variety of search options. • Different types of information, including videos, articles, games, and more. • Combination of quick facts and longer pieces. • Intuitive site for kids to learn to navigate.
Toon Book Reader www.professorgarfield.org/toon_book_reader	This site is meant for emerging readers, but because of the content, it can support a variety of learning needs.	• Options for reading aloud. • Includes comics as a genre for kids. • Addresses visual literacy skills.
Kidsreads www.kidsreads.com	This site is designed for elementary and middle school readers. It's filled with book reviews, author interviews, reading lists, and new titles.	• Allows sorting in a variety of ways. • Book reviews, interviews, announcements. • Provides a way to connect to authors with author interviews. • Updated regularly.

continued on next page

Figure 4.1. Continued.

Wonderopolis http://wonderopolis.org	Meant to foster natural curiosity and imagination for students of all ages.	• Newer Wonders have read-aloud option. • Video support. • Articles are several paragraphs and good for stamina building. • Tags and links within articles.
Discovery Education www.discoveryeducation.com	Supported by the Discovery Channel, DE uses video as its primary delivery method but also includes a variety of texts and many teacher tools.	• Variety of text reading levels and mediums. • Enables teachers to assign content to specific students based on their needs.

Fifth-grade teacher Maria Caplin shares the ways in which she used one of these sites, Wonderopolis, to demonstrate the possibilities of online reading. By having one site that she knows well, she is able to model intentional decision making in her lessons.

Voices from the Classroom

Digital Reading with Wonderopolis

Maria Caplin
Grade 5 Teacher
Bailey Elementary School
Dublin, Ohio

- How many species are endangered? (Wonder #152 http://wonderopolis.org/wonder/how-does-a-species-become-endangered)
- Who invented LEGOs? (Wonder #639 http://wonderopolis.org/wonder/who-invented-lego-blocks)
- What color is sunshine? (Wonder #116 http://wonderopolis.org/wonder/why-do-rainbows-appear)

As a classroom teacher, I am asked several inquiry questions a day. Ten years ago, I would respond, "Look it up in our class encyclopedias." More recently my response was, "Google it." Still, I wasn't always comfortable with this response because I knew the student would probably get a minimum of twenty hits and have to choose among sites to try to find the correct answer. My biggest worry was whether the student could read the information on the site well enough to answer the question. Because one of my primary concerns with digital reading is readability, I was happy to find a website that is perfect for all students because it meets the needs of most and also can be read aloud to them, which is especially important with English language learners.

I want my students to ask inquiry-based questions, and I want them to have a site that allows them to search for answers. We use Wonderopolis in our classroom as the first "go to" site if students have a question. Wonderopolis is organized in a student-friendly format that includes the following components:

- Focus inquiry question (three additional questions that will be answered in the article)
- Video that hooks students into the topic
- Differentiated vocabulary (linked to the article, including definitions)
- Focus article (additional links to further students' learning)
- Try It Out (activities that extend the Wonder of the Day)
- Test Your Knowledge (online quiz to check for comprehension)
- Wonder What's Next (opportunity to predict tomorrow's Wonder)
- Comments (students are able to leave a comment, which will be answered by Wonderopolis)

Wonderopolis is an authentic site based on common questions that students wonder about and want answers to. Students are invested in their reading when they are searching for an answer they are interested in. Students can be intentional with their reading based on their own inquiry question or a Wonder that supports classroom curriculum.

I have used Wonderopolis in all content areas, especially because I strive to integrate textbooks and reference books with digital reading as much as possible. A lesson might begin with telling students the focus Wonder question and then brainstorming together what they already know about that Wonder. I then write on chart paper their background knowledge while listening to the class conversation, which usually includes several questions students raise about the given topic. Next I display the Wonder on our SMART Board for whole-class reading, although some of the students choose to read by themselves on the classroom iPads. Depending on the focus strategy, we either read the article together or I offer to let them read silently on the iPads. As we read, students record their new learning in their spiral notebooks, and then we discuss the Wonder and answer the questions we wrote down on the anchor chart. Finally, we connect the Wonder to the standard for that day's lesson.

One of the most powerful aspects of Wonderopolis is its connectedness. First, it connects all of us in the classroom as we read and learn from the same digital text. In addition, the site lets me connect with students' families by having my students share their inquiries at home with their parents and discuss what they have learned. Typically, I assign a focus question for students to discuss with their families before writing a written response as a way to extend their knowledge. Finally, through the comment section on each Wonder students can leave a comment about their learning or ask a different inquiry question that connects to the Wonder. The Wonderopolis site always answers with an authentic, direct response, which the students are inevitably excited about.

Digital reading has changed in the past several years in my classroom. It evolves through my continued learning about sites that are student centered as well as through the opportunity to teach my students how to be intentional about the decisions they make regarding online reading. Through shared reading experiences, the students learn how to locate digital information on their own. They also learn how important it is to check the source by verifying the facts on another site as well as the vocabulary definitions by using a dictionary or another digital source. A digital text like Wonderopolis is a powerful tool that allows my students to practice and continue to be intentional with their online reading.

As we mentioned earlier, we can't rely on one tool or site if we want our students to learn intentionality. We look for sites and tools that serve a variety of learning needs. Much like Maria uses Wonderopolis, we share these sites for various reasons throughout our instruction and then use them to help build literacy skills around intentionality and decision making.

How Can Students Be Intentional about Text Choice?

One way in which readers are intentional is how they choose what to read. We want our students to know favorite authors and series. We want them to identify their individual tastes in books and have experience with a variety of genres and text types. But intentional text selection goes further than that. Our students must have search skills in order to find the information and readings they are looking for. They need to have a toolbox of websites and trusted resources they look to when making these decisions and, beyond merely knowing those websites exist, they need experience with them. It's not enough to just give students a list of links; they must be able to decipher what they need and when they need it.

One way we support kids in making intentional book choices is by sharing and curating online sources for learning more about books. Classroom Goodreads (www.goodreads.com) accounts can be used to rate books and to see what others think about a book a student might be interested in reading. Kidsreads (www .kidsreads.com) is a site packed with information on books and authors for middle grade students. New book releases, author interviews, and book reviews are all part of this site. Another popular option for kids is book trailers that can be used to help them shop for books. In the following Voices from the Classroom, Tony Keefer shares a "book hook" project that his school began as a way to build a community around books and to support students in good book choices. This work is especially valuable because, unlike the staged book trailer project we described in Chapter 3, this project is embedded in a school-wide initiative meant to give students an authentic opportunity to share a love of books and respond to their reading.

Voices from the Classroom

Book Hooks

Tony Keefer
Grade 4 Teacher
Scottish Corners Elementary
Dublin, Ohio

One of the ways I started using more technology in my reading workshop was by showing video book trailers to my students to "advertise" new books. Showing these short video previews added to students' excitement about a new book I was about to share. Our students live in a world saturated by images and videos, so it was not surprising they enjoyed most of the book trailers. Some of these trailers were fairly simple, while others were as overproduced as a Jerry Bruckheimer movie. However, something was lacking in all of the book trailers my students saw. Initially, it was difficult for me to recognize what was missing. Eventually, I realized the missing element was the personal touch of people you know sharing a book title with you.

I work hard to help my students understand that readers can be inspired to try new books when friends nudge them toward new reading adventures. Along with a daily book talk about titles that others should consider reading, a major routine in our room is sharing with a partner the books we are currently reading. Both of these strategies give students the chance to make a personal connection with books. Book talks and sharing also help to get books circulating the room. We build up some buzz for titles because we want our friends to read the books we love. It is always a joy when I confer with a student and hear, "Well, it looked interesting and Joey said I should read this book" when I ask why a particular book was chosen.

What if you could combine the power of a friendly recommendation with the power of video? You get awesomeness. If you try to make this combination work, it can be a little messy, but it is definitely worth the effort.

Our school literacy team introduced the idea of making videos for sharing books. We called these videos "book hooks." Initially, books hooks consisted of a child or pair of students filming themselves on a webcam and giving a short talk about the book and how enjoyable it was to read. After we shot these simple videos, the clips were uploaded to the library wiki so other students could watch the movies and see what books their friends from other classrooms had enjoyed.

This year my two language arts classes added some pizazz to the book hook concept. We wrote scripts and used a cheap piece of green felt to make a green screen that allowed us to drop images in the background of our movies. Some of us even secured props to facilitate the fun we had making these movies. Like the less complicated book hooks, the videos my classes made were uploaded to the library wiki so other students could be inspired to read new books.

The whole process took about two weeks. I provided a guide sheet for the content expected in the book hooks. The students wrote the scripts, found or made background images, and practiced the scripts. For the actual filming, I shot the videos using a Flip camera (the green piece of felt was hanging behind the students on the wall). We loaded the videos and background images to a library computer. Our library aide helped the kids build the videos in iMovie and upload the videos to the wiki.

We held a screening day so we could bask in our collective awesomeness and learn about some books that were not on our individual to-be-read lists. Other students in the building got to see the videos my students made by visiting the library wiki and were impressed by the work. I even shared one of the videos with the author of the book, and she sent an email to the two stars. About two weeks after we finished, both classes started asking when we would do another round.

When I think about how we can design purposeful uses of technology in a language arts classroom, I look for ideas that are authentic to the fundamental purposes of reading and writing as well as ideas that extend what children can do because of the insertion of technology. The video book hook project serves both of my major goals. Reading, understanding, and writing about a book is something we can expect most students to learn how to do well. Sharing the books we love is something we want our students to do to build lifelong reading habits. I could accomplish both of these goals without adding any technology at all. I also could add technology by making the kids compose their writing about books through word processing, or they could create a fancy visual to project behind them on the SMART Board to help them share a book with classmates. While both of these ideas expect the kids to use technology, they don't really extend what students can do. Creating a video that can be shared and enjoyed by others *does* extend what our students can do. Being able to produce a product that can be consumed and potentially inspire others is one of many reasons we should be finding ways for our kids to use technology more. When children can manipulate technology to share their learning and their world, then the insertion of technology is well worth the effort.

Tony's book hook story illustrates how students can be intentional in choosing books because of the way they connect with them. Book trailers give students that little preview into their classmates' perceptions of a book. They may not agree with the portrait a classmate paints of a book, but it can start a conversation. The book trailers that Tony describes are a good way to help students find books they love. Once students find books they love, our challenge is to help them gain the skills to read critically.

Following is the description of a lesson that Julie Johnson, an Ohio fourth-grade teacher, has done with her students to teach them about ways to critically read reliable sites. Through this lesson, her students are learning about the importance of the choices they make about what they read as well as learning to understand that not all sources are created equal.

Voices from the Classroom

Learning to Read Critically

Julie Johnson
Grade 4 Teacher
Scioto Darby Elementary
Hilliard, Ohio

How do you teach fourth graders to read critically? How do you impress upon them that just because something is written in print or online, the author isn't necessarily an expert on the subject? In today's digital world, anyone and everyone can publish their thoughts for the world to see. We've learned that with a few key words, we can search for and instantly have access to a deluge of information. Now more than ever I face the challenge of finding ways to help my young readers sift through all of this information. I need to teach them how to evaluate the quality and credibility of online resources. One of the best sites I have found to help me do this is All about Explorers (http://allaboutexplorers.com/) (Aungst and Zucker).

From the beginning, this site looks authentic. There are no ads, the list of explorers is impressive, and it includes a teacher section along with a WebQuest. In addition, the layout is easy to read, the site is easily navigated, and the antique map in the background and the Old World font add even more credibility. It's all very professional looking. When I first bring up the site, the kids are duly impressed. After I begin reading aloud, all of that changes.

I introduce the site by bringing it up on the SMART Board. We first look at Christopher Columbus's page because I know the kids have some background knowledge about him. As soon as I read the first sentence aloud, "Christopher Columbus was born in 1951 in Sydney, Australia," I hear the whispers start up.

"Huh?"

"How could he be born in 1951? That's when my grandma was born."

The room gets a little louder as the students begin to question the information I am reading. I have to quiet them down so that I can continue to read. The next few lines seem valid, and the kids read along with me silently until I get to "Columbus knew he had to make this idea of sailing using a western route more popular. So, he produced and appeared on infomercials that aired four times daily. Finally, the King and Queen of Spain called his toll-free number and agreed to help Columbus." Now the giggles begin, which quickly erupt into laughter.

"In 1942, he set sail with three ships. . . ."

"What the heck? How can he set sail in 1942 when he wasn't even born yet?"

The students know something is up at this point. We continue to read. Their protests become louder when we get to the lines "The Indians were excited about the newcomers and their gadgets. They especially enjoyed using their cell phones and desktop computers." Chaos takes over as the kids read ahead of me, noticing all of the other inaccuracies.

The ruse is up. They want to know what's going on and I let them in on the secret. This website was created by a group from Centennial School District in Pennsylvania to teach Internet literacy skills to fifth graders. It contains fake biographies about famous explorers and a series of lessons to teach students that you can't believe everything you read on the Internet.

This lesson is the start of teaching students the importance of being critical readers when conducting research. We continue by discussing the tools needed to conduct a good Internet search. We evaluate websites and other digital content together as a whole class so that eventually my students can do it independently. These lessons build the foundation for my young learners as they move forward as digital readers.

Valuing Strategic Reading

Teachers of reading have long been aware of the ways in which effective readers use strategies for understanding. Since the publication of *Mosaic of Thought* by Ellin Oliver Keene and Susan Zimmermann and *Strategies That Work* by Stephanie Harvey and Anne Goudvis, many elementary teachers have embedded strategy work into classroom instruction. These authors point out that when proficient readers read, they make connections, ask questions, visualize, infer, determine importance, and synthesize information. Harvey and Goudvis state, "Proficient readers, then, adapt strategies to their purposes for reading. But matching strategies to one's purpose requires metacognitive knowledge—an awareness and understanding of how one thinks and uses strategies in reading" (16).

As with traditional text, we want our students to be thoughtful, strategic, and intentional readers of all media. We want them to ask questions to make sense of a video or while reading a hyperlinked text. We want them to synthesize information while listening to a podcast and to annotate an ebook to remind them of their thinking later. The reading strategies we've always taught are more important than ever, but the options for how to use these strategies have expanded dramatically. We now need to talk about how to navigate a digital text and understand the attributes of these texts that are unique to the digital world. The terms listed in Figure 4.2 are ones we have grown accustomed to using at various grade levels, but we must be intentional about teaching students about these topics and helping them to navigate all the attributes. The only true way for students to understand how each works is to have experience with them in a variety of settings. Each of these elements can be introduced authentically in shared reading experiences. When students can use them naturally as readers and think about their significance and usefulness, they will quickly understand how each has the potential to enhance the reading experience.

Figure 4.2. Common online text attributes.

- **Hyperlinks (links):** While this may seem fairly simple, it's important that kids know that hyperlinks are meant to connect two different webpages and that there are a few different kinds.
  - ○ **In-text links:** those that appear in the body of a text. They are meant to help make connections between the text that students are reading and further information about that particular topic. These links are typically underlined and in a different color from the rest of the page text.
  - ○ **Navigation links:** those links that allow students to move around the site they are currently on or that link to the homepages of other sites that will provide other information about the same topic. These links are more general than in-text links.
- **Tags:** Tags are basically ways to categorize something on a fairly complex website so that it's easy for students to quickly navigate to all articles or texts on a particular topic. Not every site uses tags, but when they do they typically show up as hyperlinked words either at the beginning or end of an online text, and they can be great ways to quickly find additional information related to the topic.
- **Comments:** To engage their audience, many websites encourage readers to comment on the content of the text. These comments are meant to democratize the Web by giving readers a voice to "talk back" to the author of a piece. This is an extremely important (and often overlooked) aspect of reading on the Web. We often discount online comments as unimportant or made by those who may be uninformed, but many times comments can lead us to other opinions, ideas, and information that can be valuable. Instead of bypassing the comments because we are afraid of what might be said in them, this is another opportunity to read critically and explore point of view. There's a good chance that outside of school, students will read those comments. They must be prepared to understand who is writing them and why they exist.
- **Advertisements:** It's hard to find a website now that doesn't have advertisements. In many cases, it's difficult to tell where the content of the website ends and the advertisement begins, making it even more important to be able to identify ads on a page. Most ads identify themselves in subtle ways, with tiny text proclaiming "sponsored ad" or other strategies. Students should understand that much of the Web is driven by advertising, so we need to teach them to look for clues. Advertising online is ever changing and no strategy will work 100 percent of the time. Instead, as you work with students, focus on the difference between the purpose of an advertisement and that of the content of the page.

When students understand the decisions they can make as readers and the different ways that digital texts are constructed, they become intentional as they respond to these various types of text. In one third-grade class, two students were glued to the computers watching NFL "Plays of the Month," a video replay of the month's best plays from the NFL but animated with LEGOs. Not quite sure if what they were doing was worthwhile, I (Franki) asked the boys what they were doing. They shared the videos with me and told me that the videos were a feature on the *Sports Illustrated KIDS* site, where new ones were added each month. Reminding them that we were reading for learning, not entertainment, I asked what they were focusing on. It turns out that both boys are on the same football team and they like to watch these videos as a way to study plays.

"For example," they told me, "our coach tells us not to 'dance around' on the field. That's when we just move our feet around but don't do anything. We know not to dance around, but we don't know what we are supposed to do instead. So we've been watching these good plays and our coach is right—NFL players *never* have dancing feet. They keep moving to where they are going, but they never just move their feet around like we do. We knew what we were *not* supposed to do, but these videos helped us learn what to do instead."

These two boys were clearly using the same strategies they used in traditional texts to make sense of these videos. They had a purpose for what they were doing. They had searched and found the videos that met their purpose. They had questions they were trying to answer, and they synthesized the information from several videos to come up with an answer. All that we have learned about comprehension in traditional text transfers to our expanded definition of reading, and we love knowing that our students can be this intentional.

As part of the comprehension work shared by authors such as Stephanie Harvey, Cris Tovani, and Debbie Miller, teachers learned the importance of teaching kids to track their thinking. "These written tracks," state Harvey and Goudvis,

> help the reader monitor comprehension and enhance understanding. They also provide clues to the teacher about a reader's thinking, evidence that is difficult to ascertain without some form of oral or written response. Keeping track of thinking while reading helps students make meaning as they go. (19)

Digital tools provide many new ways for readers to intentionally track their thinking. Whether highlighting on an ebook or using digital sticky notes, our readers are still focusing on the important work of tracking their thinking to understand. However, the tools give our students more options for making sense of the text. In the next Classroom Connections, Katharine Hale shares the way her students are even more intentional with digital annotations.

Voices from the Classroom

Reading for Meaning with Digital Boards

Katharine Hale
Grade 5 Teacher
Abingdon Elementary School
Arlington, Virginia

We all love it when our students pause to jot on Post-it notes as they read. It is a powerful way for readers to make connections about characters or topics. As teachers we depend on students' note taking to determine which reading skills our students are using, confusing, or missing. But getting all students to independently jot on Post-its is never an easy task. Even when they do, we then face the challenge of keeping up with the Post-its. It seems that when sticky notes are tucked away inside pages of a book, students don't always notice patterns, overarching themes, or character development. Don't get me wrong. I still use my yellow Post-its and I typically run out of them by March. However, using what I call "digital boards" has been a game-changer for my readers.

I consider a digital board to be any virtual surface that allows a user to jot down notes and flexibly move them around. These digital boards are more commonly considered brainstorming tools and are often used by businesses because of their ability to group lots of ideas in one place. I've simply modified the purpose of these boards, but in essence they are still a place for unloading thinking. Numerous digital boards can be found both on the Web and as an app for any mobile device. Currently, those I have found useful on the Web include Lino it and Padlet. On a mobile device, Corkulous and Popplet are my favorites. But the brand of these digital boards can change over time, so our focus should never be on a specific app. It is important to learn the advantages and disadvantages of each type and then let the students decide what works best for them.

I have students who prefer digital boards that provide a simple interface. This means there is only one Post-it style, and the most you can do with it is change the color or size. Others prefer digital boards with multiple options, including index cards, arrows, checklists, and much more. Regardless of which digital board they choose, my students this year make intentional decisions about how they want to show their thinking as they read. They may decide to jot down unknown words, parts that make them wonder, details that stand out to them, or big ideas that are growing in their minds. If there is a place where students are confused about what is happening in the story, they sketch either with paper or a drawing app and insert it into their digital board. Whatever they are thinking, taking notes is a conscious and personal decision made during the reading process. Ultimately, students have found a purpose for jotting as they read. It is fascinating to watch them decide what information they want to include in their digital boards and how they want to organize the information.

I have come to realize how limited students felt in expressing their thinking when using traditional Post-its. Individual sticky notes made it difficult for readers to see text as one whole entity that grows as you read. For instance, when students came across an unknown word in a text, they would jot it down but forget to come back later to comment that reading on helped them decipher the word. Or they jotted down a character's interaction with another character but failed to notice how this type of behavior repeats later in the book. Especially for my visual and kinesthetic learners, active reading has helped them see commonalities, patterns, and changes over time in a story.

Before digital boards, I had never seen students organize Post-its independently. There was a disconnect between each of their thoughts, and bigger ideas were difficult to access. They now have a place to catch all of their thinking and make those connections. The way they now organize their thinking on digital boards gives me a window into their reading minds. Are they looking for character development? Are they noticing relationships between characters? Are they capturing the main idea? For the teacher, questions like these are much easier to answer by analyzing students' digital boards. The boards have given students choice and permission to personalize. As a result, I reap an abundance of authentic formative assessment. A digital board tells me the type of reader a student is becoming and how I can help that reader strengthen his or her reading skills.

As we have been piloting a one-to-one iPad classroom, colleagues in passing have made remarks implying that my students "probably don't know what a book looks like anymore." The truth is my students are closer to books this year than ever before. Too often people think that a digital device such as an iPad supports literacy solely because it will engage readers through ebooks or digital texts. There is certainly merit in reading ebooks and other digital texts, but if we shift our perspective on the role of digital tools, we may discover a greater impact on a student's literacy growth. The power that digital tools offer is more than the text itself. It is the ability for readers to connect to text and to develop authentic experiences with text. A digital board is a simple yet important way to impact my students' relationship and attitude toward reading.

Intentional Use of Tools

Sometimes the best strategy for a teacher is to simply get out of the way and let students make some of the decisions that might traditionally be made by their teacher. One seventh-grade English teacher that I (Bill) recently collaborated with had her students using the tools of technology for reader response. In the past, she had each student use her or his own individual notebook to respond to a shared text using a much more formulaic approach in which each student answered a similar set of questions. But she knew she wanted to give students more autonomy as the year went on, so she used various scaffolds and gradually released control of this structure to her students by introducing a variety of digital tools that would give them this independence and let them decide what works best for them.

Some of her students used Google Docs for their reader response while others used Microsoft Word, Evernote, or Etherpad. Because there are so many tools available, this teacher was able to focus less on the technology and more on her students' curricular needs. As long as their responses could be shared digitally, she didn't care what program or tool they used. What's more, she found that her students used these digital tools to help make connections through hypertext by creating links to other, related topics that helped them make sense of their own reading. Whether this was a link to Wikipedia or a YouTube video book trailer, each link helped to illustrate what students did or did not understand about a given text. Ultimately, this changed much of the way she thought about her classroom and helped her to create a more student-centered classroom.

For our students to be intentional about their work, we have to make sure our assignments do not give them conflicting messages. If we continue to give our students rubrics that ask them to cite three online sources and list those in a bibliography, they will continue to do just that. They can easily find three resources and check that off of their assignment checklist, and we can easily assess that they completed that task. However, this approach doesn't capture the thinking that needs to happen with those three resources if we want our students to make something new from the information they've synthesized. This goal is much harder to check off a list and much harder for us to assess. But even though it's more difficult, it is a much more intentional goal. It is easy to look at the new goals and standards for our students and to fall back on old practices, thus giving students the wrong message about what it means to be literate. Instead, we want students to make decisions about the things they consume and create because they want their messages to be powerful, because they want to make a difference in the world.

Digital tools give students more opportunities as readers, writers, and thinkers. Therefore, they have more decisions to make when consuming and producing information. Literacy teaching remains the same, but the new tools add new possibilities for student learning. The main real difference is that their decisions have more layers. So, if we can stay true to what we know as literacy teachers, we are really just helping our students make sense of their expanding choices.

One of the ways we try to foster finding the right tool at the right time is by empowering students to share their experiences with their classmates. In the digital age, it's not important for the teacher or the students to be familiar with every tool available. What's important is the collective knowledge of the class and the power of each student bringing his or her own strategies, understanding, and reading experience to the classroom community. Students are exposed to many tools and sites during shared reading and mini-lessons. But students are truly learning when they think about the skill that matches their purpose in their independent work. As students feel expert on a tool or site, they can add their name to a classroom chart, letting others know they are willing to share what they know. Often during workshop time, students find peer experts on a tool they need to learn and get the information they need from those experts. This helps kids be purposeful in their choice of tools, and it also values the fact that knowing a certain tool is not as important as knowing when to use the tool.

A third grader adds to our list of "I Can Teach About," adding what he can teach others in the context of literacy workshop.

As we said in the first chapter, being intentional is about making meaning-ful choices as a reader. Whether it's choosing that just-right book, deciding which device or tool to use to read or respond to a text, or, as a teacher, determining our literacy goals and then choosing the appropriate tool or method, at their core each of these has to do with making intentional decisions about the reading lives of kids.

In the next chapter, we discuss the third core feature of the digital reading workshop: connectedness. As you read this chapter, we encourage you to reflect on how making intentional decisions ties in closely with making connections to texts and, of equal importance, making connections beyond the text. How are you intentional about when you connect with others around a reading and when you don't? How are you intentional about choosing who to connect with? These are all decisions you make as a reader, no different from the decisions you make when choosing that just-right book.

What Really Matters? Connectedness

Not long ago, I (Franki) took a trip to Boston with my husband. I love the uninterrupted time on an airplane because I can catch up on my reading. At this point, the rules of "no electronics" were still in place, and I decided to put a few magazines in my bag for takeoff and landing. One of those magazines was the most recent issue of the *Horn Book*. The *Horn Book* is one of the magazines I still choose to get in paper form, and I enjoy digging into the reviews of new children's books six times a year. I like the paper version because I can fold down corners of pages discussing books I want to purchase, highlight interesting reviews, and rip out pages that I want to take with me on my next visit to the library. It seemed like the perfect magazine for the plane ride. As the plane was taking off and I began to read, however, I found myself looking for wi-fi access once we hit 10,000 feet. I quickly realized that even though I enjoy the paper copy of this magazine, my habit is to read each issue with my laptop or iPad next to me so that I can look for further information on the books that interest me. I had never just sat with the magazine and read it without popping onto the Internet to check out other reviews, visit author websites, check the ratings of my global reading network on Goodreads, ask friends on Twitter what they thought of the book, and more. Sitting there on the plane, I felt as though something was missing in my reading routine. Even though I like and use the paper copy of the magazine, my reading of it no longer exists only inside the pages of the text—it has expanded to the digital world.

Until that plane ride to Boston, I hadn't realized how much of my reading goes back and forth between tools and how many more connections I make between texts than I did a decade ago. Not only do I make connections between print and digital texts, but connecting with my global community is now a natural part of any reading experience. After this reading epiphany, I've been watching myself more closely, and I realized that whether I am reading professional journals, professional books, or entertainment magazines, I tend to read within close proximity to the Internet. This allows me to read in a sophisticated and connected way, finding various sources and synthesizing all I can. Digital tools have expanded my options as a reader, allowing me to make meaning at a higher level because of the variety of information and the multiple communities available to me.

As a reader, I can be thoughtful about my connections only because I know what is possible. I know that many of my friends read well-reviewed books, and I can find their thoughts on Goodreads and Facebook. I know many authors have websites that share reviews for their new books, and I follow many blogs and other sites that host author interviews or podcasts that always give me more information to help me make decisions about what I want to personally read or use with my students. Additionally, I often find book trailers, which help me get a feel for the tone of the book, and I know if I tweet out a question about a book, I will get several answers in a short amount of time. Because I know the possibilities and have experience with a variety of sources and networks, each decision I make to move from source to source is an intentional one.

For our students to be equally intentional as connected readers and writers, they must know what is possible in order to make those decisions. They must have experience with a variety of tools and topics and find their own sources of information that they recognize to be helpful to them as readers. Only through this intentional connectedness will students gain independence as readers as well as become more adept communicators and decision makers as they navigate their worlds both inside and outside of the classroom.

The Power of Community

As summer break begins to wind down every year, students everywhere begin to consider what the new school year will bring. In some cases, there is a sense of trepidation and anxiety, whereas in others the nervousness and excitement of beginning a new year in a new grade has them counting the days until they step back into the classroom. Children may mourn the passing of summer, but many look forward to seeing friends and experiencing the routine of a new classroom. This new beginning is not all that different for teachers. We think fondly of those first days of school when the classroom is organized, lessons are planned, and the year is full of possibilities. Inevitably that first day comes and the kids begin to file into the building. From the very beginning, as we greet that very first kid on the first day of school, we are creating connections that will carry on throughout the year. Through these simple first steps, we have already begun to build the classroom community that will live with us for the next 180 days of school and become one of the driving forces behind the learning that takes place in class. From those first moments and introductions to the seating arrangement in the classroom, each student brings a little of him- or herself, thus making up our classroom community.

As the school year begins, whether teaching third grade or eighth grade, teachers begin intentionally building their classroom community by asking students about their summers, introducing themselves, and relaying expectations and working arrangements for the classroom. While this can take time, teachers know that this work of building a classroom community is important, so we take those days and weeks to make community a part of every student's educational experience. It's worth the time.

Thinking about community and connections in this digital age is crucial because students create and connect in new and different ways. But what does it really mean to be connected as a reader in the digital age? The *NCTE Definition of 21st Century Literacies* acknowledges the importance of connectedness. For students to be literate, they need to "build intentional cross-cultural connections and relationships with others so as to pose and solve problems collaboratively and strengthen independent thought." We agree and believe that being connected is about more than sharing ideas. Being connected means that readers:

- are a part of a community of learners;
- know what resources (both people and informational) are available for learning and how to access those resources;
- can discern who (themselves included) has expertise in what areas;
- understand that members of a learning community are both learners and experts depending on the context of the learning;
- understand that learning is social;
- recognize that their thinking grows and changes because of other learners who influence them;
- know that connecting ideas is important in a learning community; and
- are intentional about making connections.

In our hyper-connected world where we seemingly have access to information at any moment, it's important to note that it's not just the act of being connected to someone else that helps us make meaning as readers. Too often we think that by creating a class blog or Twitter account we have made those connections for our students. However, lately as the two of us have begun to think about connectedness as a component of digital literacy, we realize that we have to do far more than that. We don't connect for the sake of connecting. There must be a meaningful purpose, an authenticity to it, and a diligence in our approach. For instance, Skype is a great tool for connecting with other teachers and classrooms across the world. It provides video, audio, and instant messaging, each of which is a way to connect with others. Skype even has a website (https://education.skype .com/) built specifically to provide educators a means to connect with one another through the Skype database. Truly, this is awesome, and educators from all grade levels across the world have embraced this tool. However, just because the tool exists does not mean that by Skyping with another class we can place a checkmark in front of the "making connections" list of goals and objectives we are looking to achieve with our students. The act of Skyping is merely a beginning and must be part of a greater ongoing plan that provides multiple opportunities to make connections.

We are not implying that these episodic connections are a bad thing. But it is the combined experience of many connections that becomes powerful for student learning. When used as part of a greater plan for building students' literacy skills, these connections can be a great motivator and learning experience. Consider the practice of students using video conferencing to bring into the classroom the author of a book they have just read. Students can ask questions about the author's intent and purpose, get clarifying details about specific characters, or even ask the author about her process as a writer. This interaction can give students insight into their own work as writers and help them to grow as readers. They will most certainly create a deeper understanding of the text and might even walk away with a different view of themselves as readers. These are definitely important connections, but they can't be the sole connections students make.

More important, when part of an ongoing conversation and method of instruction, the connections make a difference in the way our students approach their learning lives. When teachers are intentional about connecting their students in several ways and across several communities, students will begin to grow in ways they can't when confined to the community of the classroom. When students come to expect to connect with people and information to deepen understanding, their reading and learning change. They begin to see the unlimited possibilities for learning and can internalize it so that these practices become part of their own reading lives outside of school.

How to Support Connectedness in a Digital Classroom

So much of our work with students has always centered on the idea of community. Being connected with others for a larger purpose and being better together than we are individually has always been important for learning. But the idea of community is expanding and no longer reliant on a single location. Many of the communities we introduce our students to are still local, but these communities can also be global. To understand the idea of connectedness in a meaningful way, students must be part of a variety of communities and understand how each of these communities might interact. Students can't make sense of the importance of being connected to others if their experience with these communities is limited to the students and teachers who are a part of their classrooms.

In grades 3–8, there are many ways for students to connect beyond the classroom walls. But there are also challenges and many barriers to connecting students at a young age. We have found that students in grade 3 often have minimal experience with connecting outside of games and family conversations using tools such as Skype, FaceTime, and Google Hangouts. Their cultural backgrounds provide a good starting point, but they are just that—a starting point. By the time students are in eighth grade, we want to feel confident that they understand how to be part of and learn from and with several communities online. For this to occur, students must have experience with a wide range of purposeful connections that are focused on learning. We have found that shared experiences are often the best way to begin connecting younger students with the wider world, and the Internet provides many opportunities to connect in ways that are comfortable for teachers who are new to the global conversation.

It doesn't take much for a group of children to see the power of connectivity. One year, I (Franki) and my fourth graders participated in the annual Global Read Aloud as a way to help kids think about the world outside our four walls. This annual event is an easy way for classrooms to begin to connect because it is a short-term project. Each October students around the world are invited to participate in the event by reading the chosen book for their grade level. Then, throughout the six-week read-aloud window, classrooms connect around the book in a variety of ways. As part of our experience, we shared globally on our classroom blog. One of the things we posted was a chart of the questions we had before we began our read-aloud of *The One and Only Ivan* by Katherine Applegate. We posted the chart to our class blog and received responses from classrooms around the globe. A few days later we saw that someone who had read our blog had also tried out our idea, and we realized that we could do the same—read other postings as learners and find ideas that would stretch our thinking in new directions.

This one episode changed the way we did business in our classroom because it transformed our view of what was possible. We became more aware of how we could learn from and with others and the interactions we could have as other classrooms and students were reading our posts. The possibilities became even more evident in a quick conversation I had with Nicole about the ideas she was adding to our "Possible Blog Posts" chart. I asked her how she knew something would be a good topic for our blog, and she replied, "I think about things other schools might like to try. Like if they didn't have this idea, it would be a good idea for them. Then if they respond, we can get an idea from them. Then if we keep responding back and forth, we could all keep getting new ideas." We have found that when our students have lots of ways and reasons to connect, their stance as learners begins to change. They think hard about purpose and audience and realize that learning is never-ending. It doesn't stop when they leave the building and go home. They can continue to participate in the conversation in many different ways because they have formed connections with others. Thus they are beginning to see that they are not alone as they celebrate or struggle with texts. What's more, the personal connection they have made with the content has been strengthened because they realize they are part of a greater community of readers and learners.

There are several opportunities available for elementary and middle school classrooms to connect beyond the walls of their buildings. Some of our favorites include the following.

As we mentioned earlier, the Global Read Aloud (http://globalreadaloud .wikispaces.com) is a great way to get kids connected early in the school year. The project has grown quickly over the last few years, and the power of these connections can carry students through the year and beyond.

Another one-day event is World Read Aloud Day (http://litworld.org/ worldreadaloudday), which is sponsored by LitWorld each year on the first Wednesday of March. The focus is on advocating for literacy worldwide, and the ways in which classrooms participate are varied. Authors are often available for Skype visits and classrooms connect in multiple ways. These connections all concentrate on taking action around the idea that literacy is a right that we should celebrate and hold dear.

Additionally, each Tuesday throughout the year, the Two Writing Teachers website hosts a Slice of Life Story Challenge meme. This is an opportunity for bloggers to write and share a story about something that is happening in their own lives—a slice of the writer's life that serves as a snapshot of a specific point in time. Then in March of each year there is a Classroom Slice of Life Story Challenge (http://twowritingteachers.wordpress.com/challenges) in which readers are invited to take part in a daily (as opposed to weekly) Slice of Life writing. Classrooms across the world participate and contribute their writing and responses to the project. The power of Slice of Life is in the comments and the community. Many teachers like it because it is a short-term commitment that provides authentic audiences for our students' writing while connecting classrooms in a variety of ways. The weekly Slice of Life is a great way to build community for teachers and classrooms.

Skype is another way for students to connect outside of the classroom. On her Authors Who Skype with Classes & Book Clubs webpage (http://www .katemessner.com/authors-who-skype-with-classes-book-clubs-for-free), children's author Kate Messner helps to connect classrooms with authors by listing contact information for authors who are willing to Skype with classrooms free of charge. On her site, Kate gives tips for hosting a quality Skype session and other information on how to get started. A similar site that aims to connect authors and classrooms through Skype is called Skype an Author Network (http://skypean author.wikifoundry.com). We have found Skyping with authors to be a great way for students to see that being connected helps build understanding and also that almost no one is off limits thanks to digital tools. Authors are rock stars to our students, so when they get to talk to them via Skype, students experience the true power of connectedness.

Ongoing Opportunities for Connecting

Short-term commitments like the opportunities listed previously are easy ways to connect students with people and communities outside of the classroom. But ongoing connections are also critical if students are to truly understand the power of connectedness as readers and learners.

Blogging is a natural first step for young children, and fortunately teachers can pursue a variety of options to get them started. Teachers can embed blogging into their classroom routines and determine the best tools and audiences for connecting. Many choose a class blog using Blogger or Edublogs, where they can moderate posts and comments. Students share the experience of being part of a group blog and enjoy watching as the blog grows and changes throughout the year. Another option is for students to have their own individual blogs that are connected to a bigger classroom blog. Kidblog (www.kidblog.org) is one site we've used that gives teachers and students many options for connecting. With Kidblog, students are given their own account that is moderated by the teacher. Privacy settings are flexible, so teachers can choose to allow kids to connect only within the classroom, or they can connect with other classrooms and beyond. Because of the ability to control content in such detail, Kidblog works well with district policies and restrictions and is a comfortable place to start for many teachers.

Twitter (www.twitter.com) allows teachers and classrooms to connect around the world. Teachers with younger students often choose to set up a classroom Twitter account that the teacher manages and moderates. This allows classrooms to share globally their learning while maintaining student privacy. The main audience could be parents, other classrooms who tweet, or both. Classrooms can also connect with authors, book characters, and experts in certain fields to help lead students to a deeper understanding of what they're reading in class. A quick search will turn up a number of lists of classrooms that tweet (e.g., http://drewfrank .edublogs.org/2013/10/08/great-twitter-classroom-connections), so teachers can help students begin to follow and learn from a few specific people or groups.

Goodreads (www.goodreads.com) is a social network for readers to share, review, and discuss the books they read, much like they would with friends or family, but online and with a bigger community. To have an individual account, readers must be thirteen years of age, so this is another site where teachers of students younger than thirteen can create a classroom account and model good digital citizenship practices with their students. Through Goodreads, classrooms can share their reading, rate and review books, and learn from others. Recently, a readers' social network for children called BiblioNasium (www.biblionasium.com) has been created that allows students to have their own accounts to track their reading and to review and recommend books. Additionally, several school library systems such as Follett's Destiny (www.follettsoftware.com) have built-in social networks for readers to do similar things. Giving students the ability to connect with readers in a social way helps to establish effective reading habits in readers of all ages, and these tools allow teachers to create opportunities to connect around books in a variety of ways.

Digital tools can also be used to connect readers within the classroom community. Fifth-grade teacher Scott Jones uses digital bulletin boards to connect students' thinking during read-aloud.

Voices from the Classroom

Digital Bulletin Boards

Scott Jones
Grade 5 Teacher
J. W. Reason Elementary
Hilliard, Ohio

"Mr. Jones, can't you stop talking and spend more time just reading?" Colin interrupted during a discussion about our class read-aloud, *The False Prince* by Jennifer Nielsen. "We spend so much time talking about the book that we don't get through enough each day."

"What do you mean?" I asked him with a puzzled expression.

"Well, I like talking about this book and all because it's a little difficult for me to understand. But then we always spend too much time talking and not enough time reading," Colin clarifies as he picks the plastic off his shoelace. "No offense."

"None taken, Colin. You're right." As I continued to read the words on the page, I was really thinking about how we do spend lots of time making connections and inferences during read-aloud time. But read-aloud is supposed to be interactive. When we discuss, it helps readers understand the text. "What do you want me to do, send a text message with a question?" I said jokingly.

"Yeah!" shouted the students.

Read-aloud time seems to be the most coveted part of our daily reading workshop. My fifth graders, no matter their reading level, cannot get enough of this shared reading experience. But Colin really made me think. *Is there a way to create a place for students and me to discuss our reading lives? What kinds of tools are out there so everyone can participate in this discussion?* After spending time on Twitter with a few members of my personal learning network, I realized there is a way to create a digital dialogue where students can share their thinking and extend their learning. I started to think of all the possibilities this could offer in addition to read-aloud.

Digital bulletin boards are now where my students and I not only keep track of our learning but also *extend* our learning beyond the physical classroom space. We use these boards to nurture our classroom culture of reading and writing. We engage in a conversation about our reading lives. We make connections between reading and writing mini-lessons, share book recommendations, brainstorm possible themes of our class read-aloud, share our struggles as readers, and talk about our favorite sentences from mentor texts. These digital bulletin boards have allowed us to have an authentic discourse about our literacy experiences.

There are a few great digital corkboards out there, but I find the website most effective in meeting my students' needs is Padlet. Padlet is a free website/application where you can create an online bulletin board to display information, a wall where students post notes and add multimedia such as text, images, files, links, and videos. The settings allow you to make your wall open to the public, completely private, or moderated by you where posts require your approval. Once your wall is established, you have a digital platform for students to instantly create and collaborate on content in real time. Students create, update, and view others' notes instantaneously. Best of all, Padlet allows you to embed the bulletin board into your own website, so students don't have another login page to visit.

To introduce digital bulletin boards to my students, I use my daily reading workshop mini-lesson. I start out the cycle of mini-lessons by explaining my vision for these boards—to extend our culture of wild reading into the home. I spend one to two mini-lessons showing Padlet and sharing its many features. The last few mini-lessons are used to brainstorm possible response topics and to model quality responses with a 160-character limit. For the first few weeks, I give students a specific prompt or question to guide their thinking. For many of my students, this is enough support, and they begin to ask, "Do we have to answer your prompt, or can we just write what we want?"

After this mini-lesson cycle, students are off and creating digital content to share with one another. Each week I use Padlet to create a new bulletin board, which I embed into my classroom website (www.theflockjwr.com). Students have opportunities to post during reading workshop time, or they can post at home. While I don't assign traditional homework, I do ask students to contribute to a digital bulletin board every week. After a few weeks of using our digital bulletin boards and enjoying the subsequent discussions they generate, students see the importance of them to our reading community; therefore, most students complete them at home without any hassle.

Not only has it enhanced students' discussion about their reading, but the bulletin board has also been a great tool for quick formative assessment. I can briefly check in to see if my students have reached their reading learning targets.

So what are some examples of content we can add to our digital bulletin boards? Students can:

- Share new knowledge or understandings learned in any content area
- Draw connections to previous learning
- Write a summary of their reading that day
- Raise questions they still have about a text
- Share "a-ha" moments during independent reading

The more years that I teach students like Colin, the more I want to knock down my classroom walls. As a teacher in a self-contained fifth-grade classroom, I want to smash the barriers that separate content areas. Learning should not take place in isolated silos. That's why I aim to create a wide-open space for a more integrated reading experience for my students. Plus, much to Colin's delight, it allows me to read aloud longer. In the age of social media and digital learning, tearing down these walls is easier than ever before. Using Padlet to create digital bulletin boards has been a simple, accessible activity that can demolish the walls that separate students while also building a culture of lifelong readers and learners.

Through tools such as Padlet, Twitter, Goodreads, and many others, we have opportunities to teach kids about community and help them to experience the power of connectedness. By intentionally creating *several* different options for kids to connect throughout the year, we have found that students change their stances as readers and writers. They begin to see connecting as a natural part of their reading, writing, and learning, and they begin to expect to learn *with* the world and not just *about* it.

Connected Reading

The power of the connectedness that digital tools provide is important beyond the level of community. Our students do become part of networks that enhance their lives as readers, but they also have the tools at their fingertips to connect their reading to other reading in order to deepen their individual understanding. We know from the NCTE policy research brief on reading that "reading comprehension results from the integration of two models, text-based and situation based" (x). If we don't stay focused on this duality, our students will begin to see reading as a series of isolated text-based events that seldom come together. Connected reading, in contrast, suggests that students use multiple sources to comprehend more deeply. One requirement of the Common Core State Standards (CCSS), for example, is that students read multiple texts on a single topic. Beginning in grade 3, our students are asked "to compare and contrast most important points and key details presented on the same topic" (National Governors Association Center for Best Practices, and Council of Chief State School Officers). This is another way of saying that reading should not be done in isolation but rather as a means to explore information and multiple viewpoints that are connected by a single topic. When we provide this opportunity, students learn to explore and identify the connections between the texts and, in turn, we can allow them to learn from one another and the communities we've created.

We do not want our students to be passive consumers of content. Instead, we want them to dig in for understanding and to know which tools and resources will help them make meaning. Sometimes that means connecting with a community to hear other points of view. Sometimes it means finding other resources to extend thinking. Just as Franki intentionally moves from her *Horn Book* reading to other sites where she can find different thinking on the books reviewed, we want our students to move in and out of texts when digging for understanding and to make intentional decisions as they seek additional information and opinions.

As readers, we can no longer rely on one source of information as the end-all for understanding. Instead, it is important that our students read beyond a single text in all content areas. Initially when we used online resources, we read or shared them as we would a print resource. We didn't talk about which links to use, we didn't look at tags, we didn't follow up by adding the comment stream to our understanding. Our prior experience in working with text was clouding our use of these more flexible texts. Now we understand that all of these pieces work together for understanding, and if we want our students to be active consumers of information, we need to create opportunities for these connections to happen seamlessly in our classrooms.

Katherine Sokolowski wants her students to see the power of connecting different texts on the same topic. She is thoughtful about the text and video pairings she introduces to students, knowing this will invite them to do similar connecting in their independent reading.

Voices from the Classroom

Video as Paired Texts

Katherine Sokolowski
Grade 5 Teacher
Washington Elementary
Monticello, Illinois

My students today inhabit a world much different from the one I grew up in during the 1970s and 1980s. Their world is visual and, somehow, smaller. When I was growing up, problems occurring across the world were far from my mind. I had no connection to the kids who inhabited those countries and couldn't imagine what their lives were like. My students can. Within minutes I can call up a photo, an article, or a video to take my students to another spot on the globe. We can learn what daily life is like in Australia, ride on a camel's back in India, or take in the skyline from the London Eye. The world is open to them, which has benefits across all subjects. In particular, I have found that incorporating video has a huge impact in reading workshop.

I have long used paired texts for students to compare. We look at similar themes, story lines, and characters and write about them. While the students enjoy this, I find they are even more engaged when one of those "texts" happens to be a video. Here are just a few of the texts and videos I have paired up in our reading class to activate background knowledge before reading.

- **Excerpts from *Trash* by Andy Mulligan and this video from Louis Cole:** https://www.youtube.com/watch?v=yFnbzGrxiY8 (we watched from the beginning to 6:10): The horrific life described in *Trash* of making a living scavenging in a dump is almost incomprehensible to my students. Seeing Louis Cole visit a place in Africa that is similar to the setting in *Trash* helped my students understand the setting of the novel before beginning the text.

- **Wonderopolis** is a website that does an amazing of job pairing video and text, but sometimes I pick alternate videos. For one of their articles on murmuration (http://wonderopolis.org/wonder/what-is-a-murmuration), I used the following video to activate knowledge of the topic before we began: https://www.youtube.com/watch?v=iRNqhi2ka9k (Clive and Smith). My students had not heard of the term *murmuration* before. After watching this video, they had a clear understanding of the concept and its beauty.

We typically watch the video, pause, take a few notes, and then read the text, annotating as we go. Every time we have conducted a lesson this way, the students tell me they understand the subject more deeply because they "saw" it first.

I also connect reading and video to explore a theme, such as pairing the picture book *The Dot* by Peter Reynolds and this video from Nike on the idea of "greatness": https://www.youtube.com/watch?v=zyfU6pTLrOU&. We read the picture book, watch the video, and take notes: What does greatness mean to us? What does it mean to *make your mark*? In groups, students find ways they want to extend their thinking—creating a video response, an audio response using Audioboo, or a written response they share with the class.

We also can find videos to continue our thinking about a nonfiction topic. When my students and I shared Brenda Guiberson's *Frog Song* this year, they were fascinated—and horrified—by the Darwin's frog. To continue their learning, I purchased *The Mystery of Darwin's Frog* by Marty Crump. Still, they wanted more. They needed to *see* the frog in action. So I found a video of the Darwin's frog by National Geographic: http://video.national geographic.com/video/weirdest-darwins-frog. With their knowledge gleaned from the books and the actual video clip of the frog, my students had a deeper understanding of the life of these frogs.

Books can take us to other worlds. Our imagination is strong enough to conjure great visuals of what we read. That doesn't mean we should discount the power of a short video clip. With my students, I have found that a quick clip increases their engagement, comprehension, and desire to learn more. So often in class I find that by pairing videos with text, my students go on to research more on their own later. That should be the goal of any good workshop—creating independent lifelong learners. Videos help lead my students in that direction.

Digital Text Sets as Shared Reading

One important paradigm shift in this connected thinking is to move beyond the mere acquisition of knowledge; instead, we want our students to build deep understandings around concepts and ideas and then adopt these ideas as they read independently. Connected reading builds this understanding. When kids learn to connect their reading to other texts or people and to move beyond that initial, single text because they want to understand more deeply, they realize that community and connectedness are bigger than a group of people. Rather, they are a way of thinking and being active in all that we consume and create.

Connectivity with resources starts with being thoughtful about the resources we use across content areas. Rather than choosing texts and resources that *teach* about a topic, we want to build digital text sets that help students *explore* an idea. For a third-grade social studies unit on community, for example, I (Franki) wanted students to move beyond a superficial, dictionary-definition-level understanding of community. I wanted them to understand that community is about people and interconnectedness. I wanted to build understanding, not merely share content. So I set out to create what I call a "digital text set." Instead of the traditional text set, in which I collect several books to build understanding on a topic, I collected a variety of texts to build understanding through a shared reading experience across several days. I didn't merely choose the resources that popped up when I Googled "community." When I did that, the list that appeared included several informational pieces that offered little room for independent thinking and connecting ideas.

On the first day, I shared two separate pieces with the students. I wanted them to reframe their thinking a bit to consider what makes a community work. I told them I was going to share two texts as part of our discussion about community and then we'd talk about how these texts added to their understanding of what makes a community. These two pieces provided an amazing conversation about community and what it means to be part of a community. One was a video about a boy who makes a difference (www.youtube.com/watch?v=t3DDjeVeJu4) by encouraging others and leading in spite of his age ("Tree"). Following that, I shared a simple picture book called *The Little Hummingbird* by Michael Nicoll Yahgulanaas about a little bird who makes a difference in his community.

The next day we read the picture book *What If Everybody Did That?* by Ellen Javernick and Colleen M. Madden. This was a quick read that reminds us why we have rules by taking readers into different settings, thinking about not following a rule, and asking, "What if everybody did that?" We then talked about all of the communities we are a part of and how each has its own goals, rules, etc. Kids mentioned school, sports teams, churches, neighborhoods, our city, and other aspects of communities and made personal connections with their own experiences and thinking.

On the third day of our ongoing conversation around community, I paired two more videos to help students continue to extend their thinking. I wanted to focus on the idea of a learning community instead of a general community and how members of a community support one another in a variety of ways. The first video was an amazing production from Pernille Ripp's fifth-grade classroom: *My Students' Classroom Vision* (http://pernillesripp.com/2013/09/09/my-students-classroom-vision-2). In the video, each of Pernille's students shares goals they have for the year and how they plan to be brave as learners in a community of learners. It was a powerful experience for my kids because they could identify with it and thus it became personal for them. We followed up with a conversation about being brave, being part of a learning community, individual goals, and community goals. I shared my own experiences about how easy it is for me to meet a reading goal because I love to read, but it was brave of me to set a running goal and to put myself out there when running is something I have to work hard at and be vulnerable with. We talked about how the book I am writing has been hard for me lately and it takes being brave to not just quit. We continued to discuss how it's easier to help one another be motivated to meet our goals when we know what other people's goals are (as in any community). Our discussion was very informal but at the same time very thoughtful.

I followed up with a clip that I love of Kristin Chenoweth (www.youtube .com/watch?v=FpXm_sXcc_Y) ("For Good"). I chose this piece because I wanted students to see that communities can celebrate one another. We talked about how Kristen Chenoweth was so good at her craft and how she celebrated a guest singer who joined her on stage and turned out to be amazing. As her guest sang, Chenoweth cheered for her and was so happy to be sharing the stage with her. We talked about how that says a lot about Chenoweth and shows that she loves seeing others do well and succeed. Almost immediately kids began talking about ways they support others and cheer them on when they are successful. They were as interested in Chenoweth as they were in the friends of the guest singer who must have been filming and cheering throughout the performance.

On the final day of our extended conversation, I concluded this exploration of community through a digital text set with *Austin's Butterfly* (http://vimeo .com/38247060) (Berger), a video demonstrating the power of a classroom community and highlighting the way that the kids in the video supported and thought through the story the teacher was sharing.

Through this digital text set, I was able to reach several goals I had for and with my students. It helped me think differently about how I was sharing content with my students, and it helped them see that as readers, we build understanding as we read, view, and connect one piece with others. They saw the continued connections and recognized that each of these pieces did not exist solely in isolation but were stronger together. We explored the emotion of music and the empathy of a told story and expanded our thinking around the topic of community. Because of the medium of the texts I chose, students had a different relationship with the texts and developed a deeper understanding of what it means to be part of a community.

Connecting Text with Digital Tools

Digital tools make it easy for readers to collect digital texts on a specific topic. If we teachers share our own collection process, create opportunities in shared reading, and invite students to read in connected ways, our students will learn to do this naturally themselves. To begin, we take advantage of students' natural curiosities to help them explore connected reading on an individual level. One year a group of Franki's students was fascinated by Winter the dolphin. They had read *Winter's*

Tail: How One Little Dolphin Learned to Swim Again by Juliana Hatkoff, Isabella Hatkoff, and Craig Hatkoff, a story that follows the journey of a baby dolphin who was rescued from a trap. This group showed an authentic interest in the topic, so I searched for and found several other pieces that might connect to this reading. I knew that Google and other search engines often produce so many results that the search for connected articles becomes cumbersome and frustrating for young children. I wanted to circumvent that frustration, and I knew there were tools that could collect and share kid-friendly texts that were connected in some way.

For this particular group of students, I digitally bookmarked a variety of resources for them to explore on the topic of Winter the dolphin. When I bundled the set of resources, my goal was to include a variety of texts and medium types. I wanted my students not only to integrate information from several sources, but also to see the variety of ways in which people share information to learn about a topic.

As students begin to read more informational text, I want them to discover new questions and interests to continue expanding their thinking. I want them to see how researching and learning about one topic typically raises interest in other topics that may be related. In this case, in addition to links specific to Winter the dolphin, I included links to related topics such as dolphins in general and prosthetics use in animals, hoping to foster more curiosity beyond a simple understanding of the plot of the story. My curated site of links comprised a variety of media and content types, including a newspaper interview with Winter's trainer, a live webcam into Winter's current home at the Clearwater Aquarium, a YouTube video chronicling Winter's progress from rescue to the present, a virtual field trip to the aquarium where Winter lives, a news article on a children's news site about the movie about Winter, a Wonderopolis post on how dolphins and porpoises are different, a link to facts about bottlenose dolphins, and a slideshow about other animals that use prosthetics. With all of these resources together in one space, my students were able to read, watch, and connect with a multitude of texts.

This same activity could be implemented at any grade level with any topic. In this case, I curated the sites to make it easier for the group to find and use the information. In older grades, my curation efforts would not be as extensive because I would work with the students to help them complete their own searches and curate their own links for themselves and to share with one another. The power of this learning comes in the connections made across digital text sets and the community of learners that can be created as students connect to different texts around the same topic.

In one seventh-grade class that Bill worked with, the teacher wanted students to do collaborative research around the general topic of social justice. Students were reading *Lockdown* by Walter Dean Myers, and the teacher was looking for ways to help them connect with other types of texts around that same topic. Because we were working with seventh graders, the teacher also wanted to give students experience with online searching, annotation, and collaboration as they worked with the content. To facilitate this, each student set up a Diigo (www.diigo .com) account as well as an account for the now discontinued Google Reader (any RSS feed will do, though). After a few mini-lessons on effective search skills and using Diigo to bookmark, annotate, and share a webpage, students began their search for digital texts that informed their thinking about the topic related to social justice that their group had chosen. As they found articles, videos, pictures, and audio clips, students annotated and bookmarked the site to share with their class-mates. Through Diigo's RSS feature, students subscribed to the stream of infor-mation each of their classmates had created, so everyone had the same content to read, watch, or listen to. Over time, this content became the focus of their in-class, small-group discussions as they continued to expand their understanding of the topic. Students were not only finding connections between texts for themselves, but they were also relying on their classroom community to help them gain deeper understandings. Only through these digital tools could students efficiently and ef-fectively share the content they found.

One of our goals for students is to have them connect print and digital resources in their reading lives. Fifth-grade teacher Karen Terlecky achieved this by using the QR code tool to connect students with sources for book previewing. Tools like this help students make these connections while deciding what to read.

Voices from the Classroom

QR Codes to Support Book Choice

Karen Terlecky
Grade 5 Teacher
Glacier Ridge Elementary
Dublin, Ohio

I am fortunate to have a variety of technological tools in my classroom (iPads, laptops, and desktops) as well as a BYOD policy. This allows us great flexibility in the ways we learn as individuals.

But no matter how many wonderful tools we have, for me it always comes back to the question of what is the most important thing I want students to learn.

Recently I noticed that, as students had grown as readers through the year, they were having a more difficult time with self-selection of books. Many students had been reading one type of book for so long that when it came time to push themselves to the next level, they didn't have the skill set to do so.

We had talked all year long about how, in addition to classmates' recommendations, browsing was important in book selection—reading the back cover or book flap and trying out a few pages of the first chapter to determine whether the book matched what they were looking for in their next book. But even with those tools, some students still could not find the right book for them.

So, looking at my classes' needs, I decided to focus on self-selection as our goal.

After recently hearing Kristin Ziemke (one of the authors of *Connecting Comprehension and Technology* [Harvey, Goudvis, Muhtaris, and Ziemke]) speak about her first graders creating book reviews and then turning them into QR codes to place in the books, I realized something like this would work for my fifth graders as well, and might give them a few more tools to help with their self-selection.

Our mini-lessons in reading workshop for a week were about the topic of self-selection. Some of the lessons were review and others pushed students to look at a book in more depth as they were making reading decisions. I showed book trailers, we looked at authors' webpages, and we read reviews of books.

This was setting the stage for what I asked students to do next. They chose a book they loved and thought other classmates would enjoy reading, researched it (book trailers, reviews, authors' webpages, and, in some instances, book or book series webpages), and eventually wrote a personal review of the book. The end goal was to have fifty books (one from each of my students) with additional information to support readers in their self-selection.

So my language arts goals were clear: book selection, research, review writing.

But to get to the end, we needed a few technology skills to help us. We needed to learn how to do smart searches when looking for information about a book, we needed to review how to make a video or audio clip using QuickTime for our personal reviews, and we had to learn how to make QR codes with the links we found in our research and the links students would create for their reviews.

With assistance from one of our technology support teachers, the students were paired with a partner, and they moved into the work of researching, culling the best information to support the book, making audio or video clips of their book reviews, and translating all of this into individual QR codes.

Our workshop hummed with the busy work of readers with a purpose. The work they did collaboratively was brilliant. Though my plan for pairing them had more to do with number of devices available, it turns out that having to go through this learning process twice, first for one book and then for the partner's book, was invaluable. The collaborative talk and discussions in the room as students made decisions about what "made the cut" to become a QR code was amazing. It really helped them filter through what seems like a fun website versus what really helps readers.

The collaboration was equally essential during the videotaping with QuickTime, as students problem-solved how to display the book properly, adjusted the sound, listened to what they had created, and revised the product if it wasn't quite right.

For now, all fifty books are sitting on a shelf called "Books You Just Can't Miss." It is delightful to see the readers who were hesitant with book selection just a few short weeks ago taking a device over to the bookshelf to scan the QR codes to gather more information before making a book selection decision.

Tools That Connect Texts

Just as baskets help us collect books and articles of traditional resources in our rooms, a variety of tools can help us invite students to think beyond a single text. Some of our favorite tools (see Figure 5.1) for facilitating this invitation are Symbaloo and QR codes. Each of these tools scaffolds the integration of information for students without taking away the choice and decision making of kids searching for what they want to read or the information they hope to find.

Figure 5.1. Some of the authors' favorite tools for helping students think beyond a single text.

Tool	Description
QR codes www.qrstuff.com www.beetagg.com	QR codes are barcodes that can be read by a camera on a mobile device and contain information that connects digital pieces to texts. Many teachers and librarians create QR codes that link to a website and place them on related books. Some teachers also make sheets of QR codes that students can choose from when reading on a topic. They can be used in many ways, but in this case, a physical barcode connected to a virtual bookmark can help students make connections between texts.
Symbaloo www.symbaloo .com	Symbaloo is a visual social bookmarking site. You can build a Symbaloo webmix/page that contains a number of different bookmarks and organize them by topic. A Symbaloo page gives you room for a great number of sites, and it also allows you to organize them visually by color and icon so they are easy for readers to find.
Diigo www.diigo.com	Diigo is another social bookmarking site that allows you to save and tag a Web resource to access at a later time. These tags and lists of resources can then be shared with others via a website for that tag or an RSS feed that will syndicate all new bookmarks, allowing others to subscribe to the feed.
Feedly (RSS reader) www.feedly.com	Feedly is an RSS (really simple syndication) reader that allows you to subscribe to a stream of digital information and aggregate any post or bookmark that has been subscribed to. Because it brings all of the information into one space, it's an easy way to gather information and stay updated when doing a collaborative project.

While it's often said that the tool doesn't matter, we believe that the range of tools teachers choose matters a great deal. Without digital tools like those listed in Figure 5.1, the curating and sharing of information would be far more tedious and the process would get in the way of consuming, synthesizing, and understanding information. In our examples, the tools are not the focus, but they are necessary to create the connections between people and between texts that are crucial to gaining a deeper understanding of a given topic. By connecting with texts (both print and digital) and to resources beyond the classroom walls, our students' reading and understanding become more sophisticated.

We believe strongly that if we create classrooms where reading is authentic, where students are connected to one another and to the world, and where students make intentional decisions as readers, we have created environments in which readers in this digital age can thrive. In the remainder of the book, we explore ways to continue to build on the classroom environment, incorporate digital assessment practices, and more effectively involve the community in digital reading practices.

Assessment: Keeping Our Eye on the Literacy

Assessment needs to be the vehicle that moves us beyond defining our readers as a number. Assessment should not be about defining a reader but about piecing together information to help us design classroom experiences so we can observe our readers learning and understand what each one needs.

—*Assessment in Perspective*, Clare Landrigan and Tammy Mulligan

My (Franki's) fourteen-year-old daughter, Ana, decided to teach herself Minecraft last summer. She quickly became addicted and did all she could to learn to play the game well. At first she just jumped in and played, and as she met obstacles, she stopped to learn what she needed to know. During her monthlong addiction to learning Minecraft, she used a variety of reading and problem-solving strategies, including:

- Watching YouTube tutorials and applying the information while playing
- Texting friends who currently play Minecraft
- Teaching friends new to Minecraft how to play
- Reading a (paper) book on Minecraft
- Finding and bookmarking links that she wanted to revisit to learn from

As a mom thinking about digital literacy, I recognized the purposefulness of much of what Ana was doing and marveled at how efficiently she was doing it. She was able to use multiple tools to find information. She knew her purpose when researching and could easily find the resources that would help her. She moved easily between a variety of tools (paper book, iPhone, laptop) and types of media, and she was clearly able to navigate the information once she found it. Some of her research was formal and some was more informal, in the form of conversations with friends. She was asking her own questions, navigating Web-based resources easily, and she was able to pull out important information based on her needs.

When I listened in and watched as the teacher-mom that I am, I noticed all of the things Ana was doing well as a reader. Many of the skills we listed in the first chapter of this book were evident in Ana's Minecraft adventure—annotating, reading across texts, determining importance, connecting and synthesizing, monitoring comprehension, repairing meaning, knowing where to go, asking questions, sharing in multiple ways, changing thinking. Had I been her teacher, I could have taken notes, screen shots, videos, etc., to document her growth as a digital reader and her effective research skills. I would have had evidence of many of the listed behaviors and gotten a good assessment of where Ana was as a reader and where she might go next in her learning. At the same time, I realized how different this assessment was from the ways we assess our students in schools. No one told Ana how many resources she had to have. No one told her she had to consult one paper resource and one online resource. No one gave her specific questions to answer, and she took no notes on the research she conducted. Yet she was capable of asking her own questions and finding the answers as they suited her.

Like many teachers, we have struggled with finding the best ways to conduct assessment in a digital reading workshop—because of both the disconnect between the kinds of school assessment that seem to "count" and the current buzz around digital assessment. In our conversations with teachers and administrators around the country, the general feeling is that teachers are collecting information on the technology rather than the reading. Somehow, with the inclusion of digital tools, it's easy to move away from the things we know to be true of literacy assessment. But in this digital age, we both believe that we must keep our eye on the literacy and assessment practices we have trusted for years.

Starting the Year

If we want to assess students in authentic ways, as we have always tried to do, it is important that we think about our beginning-of-the-year assessments. For years, I (Franki) have given a reading interview to each child during the first few weeks of school. I have a list of questions that I ask students in order to start a yearlong conversation about their reading. This interview serves as my first assessment as I learn about tastes, behaviors, and habits. I realized recently that my beginning-of-the-year reading assessment also sends my students a message about the kinds of reading that are valued in the classroom. The questions I ask set the stage for what my students come to expect as readers. In the past, I have asked questions such as these:

- What types of books do you like?
- What types of books do you not like?
- Is there a series that you enjoy?
- Where do you read?
- When do you read?
- Who do you talk to about books?
- What kinds of things do the people in your family read?
- Who is your favorite author? Why?

My interview questions focused on more traditional reading and traditional text; I didn't include any questions about digital reading. So I revised and added the following questions to begin my assessments this fall. My new questions include:

- How often do you read each day? (Don't count only book reading.)
- What do you know about the ways you can read other than paper books?
- Do you usually read paper books or other types of books? Explain.
- What kinds of things do you read online or on a computer/phone/tablet?
- Do you read any blogs or websites on a regular basis? If your answer is yes, how often?
- What kinds of things do your family members read?
- Do you read on any type of e-reader?
- Have you read anything that includes other types of media (e.g., video) as part of the story?
- Have you ever read an audiobook?
- What do you think is a challenge of online reading?
- What are some things you are curious about when it comes to reading today?

By adding these questions, I not only get to know the digital reading experiences of my students, but I also let my students know that I believe reading includes more than traditional texts.

Structures for Ongoing Assessment

Workshop teaching has always stressed how important it is to sit next to a child and talk about her or his reading life. Workshop teachers have always observed students and listened in on book club conversations. We have always analyzed the tracks of their thinking while they are reading, and our conference notes often give us insight into where to go next. None of this changes with digital tools. We assess digital literacy as we have always assessed print-based literacy. We rely on the structures and routines we have always had in place so that we can help students make informed decisions about their reading. These structures may include:

- Kidwatching
- Taking notes while conferring
- Analyzing written responses
- Examining student annotations
- Listening in on conversations
- Analyzing miscues and oral reading
- Talking to students about their own goals
- Collecting artifacts and written responses to reading
- Synthesizing use of strategies for understanding

Solid literacy assessment remains the same with or without digital tools. According to the NCTE Position Statement *Formative Assessment That* Truly *Informs Instruction*:

> Formative assessment is a constantly occurring process, a verb, a series of events in action, not a single tool or a static noun. In order for formative assessment to have an impact on instruction and student learning, teachers must be involved every step of the way and have the flexibility to make decisions throughout the assessment process. (3)

We believe strongly in this stance and agree that our assessment techniques should be about moving readers forward in their learning. The digital tools we use have not changed these beliefs. Rather, they have given us better tools with which to monitor and encourage the journeys of our readers.

Gretchen Taylor, a seventh-grade teacher when she shared the following anecdote, used observation and informal assessments during an inquiry unit in her language arts class. Instead of focusing on isolated skills, she embedded the tools and strategies into authentic inquiry.

Voices from the Classroom

Learning from Experts

Gretchen Taylor
Grade 7 Language Arts Teacher
Sells Middle School
Dublin, Ohio

In this year's most research-heavy unit, my teaching partner and I framed students' inquiries around two options, one of which was the hot topic of innovation. We framed the unit in this way:

> What are traits of innovators in your field? Study the history of your field of choice and look for threads of the traits/habits of innovators in the field. Then study a current person in the field, interviewing him or her to trace the threads to the present. Finally, suggest one idea for an innovation that is needed in your field.

Our requirement for digital composition pointed students toward very intentional digital reading, as well.

Each of our young writers started with a general inquiry, and each discovered through deep digital reading innovations that were fine-tuned to their interests and the interests of their seventh-grade peers.

The first inquiry Morgan reported to me on our Google Forms check-in was this: "How have people been innovative with athletics programs?" As my teaching partner and I circulated through our media center and conferred with other students about their reported inquiries, I noted Morgan back in the computer lab, intensely focused on her screen, clicking through links and occasionally typing into her search engine.

"Morgan, tell me more about your athletics inquiry," I gently interrupted.

"Actually, I've narrowed it down to innovation in soccer," Morgan told me. "And I found on other websites some ideas about how soccer is innovative, so I'm going to keep reading."

"So far, have you noticed any trends in what the sites have mentioned about innovations?" I asked.

Morgan's eyes lit up. "Well, actually, one thing I noticed is this thing called a Soccket—" she pointed at her screen, showing a picture of a soccer ball with a light jutting out of it—"which popped up on one of my search results when I dug into my list of links. I'm not sure if it fits the prompt, though."

"It definitely looks intriguing," I responded, "so I'm going to give you time to keep reading and thinking. I'll check in with you tomorrow to see where your reading has taken you."

Morgan emailed us that night asking us to read a draft of an inquiry she'd composed to the inventors of the Soccket:

> [At first] I looked at [the Soccket] and I was confused. I showed my friends and we were both like, "What is that?" As I continued to look at the Soccket, it made me more and more curious. I looked up [an] article on

the internet, and had good results. I was becoming fascinated by the fact that a small soccer ball could give so much to people that have so little. The people in Nigeria and Mexico, are being benefitted, from playing and having fun. I think that is really great. As I was looking deeper into the topic, I came to the conclusion that, this is innovation!

I was wondering:

- In what other ways do you view the Soccket as innovative?
- Have you ever considered your design as innovative?
- How big of an impact does the Soccket have on the underprivileged countries?

These are just some of my questions and I would love if you could answer them!

Over the days that followed, Morgan continued to read and to use information from her wide digital reading, as well as information she received in response to her email inquiry (after one false start when she received an auto-reply about employment opportunities!), to create a meaningful digital piece rooted in her very intentional digital inquiry into an innovation she'd come to love.

Through my observations, I learned the following about Morgan as a reader:

- She is **dynamic**—Morgan bookmarked, rather than printed off, her texts, so she frequently revisited her texts and could interact with them differently each time based on her purpose. Further, because the reading process remained open, Morgan didn't prematurely settle for a topic less suited for our and her established purpose.
- She is **interactive**—Morgan freely linked in and out of her sources to broaden and narrow the scope of her topic as she researched.
- She is (unexpectedly) **connected**—Morgan stayed plugged into her inquiry and, encouraged by the digital element of the "contact us" form, she took the opportunity to directly interact with the creators of the innovation.

I was struck by one word in particular in Morgan's author's note: "[Her original] idea transitioned into innovation in soccer, which blossomed into innovation within the Soccket." *Blossomed.*

One challenge with assessments in the digital age is that we must ensure we are assessing student growth as readers and writers rather than assessing isolated technology skills. Sticking with the routines and structures we've known to be effective helps us to do just that. We do not give up what we already know about what works when assessing literacy skills; rather, we hold true to the strategies and practices that we know work with readers and provide students with the tools—digital and nondigital—they need to be successful communicators. However, we must at the same time incorporate new assessment strategies that honor the work done by students in these new mediums and formats.

Tools That Help with Assessment in a Digital Age

Digital tools give teachers and students ways to assess growth that were not available only a few years ago. Instead of taking notes of all that was observed and discussed, with digital tools we can gather real artifacts from a child's learning and collect and organize the artifacts over time. There may be times when we want to record an oral reading on paper, but at other times, we will want to record the audio of a child reading a page from a book, and perhaps include a photo of the page. This gives us not only more information than the written record, but also something that a child can reflect on more easily. It is now possible to assess literacy using a variety of digital tools, and more are released every day. Some of our favorite tools for assessing students' reading are listed in Figure 6.1.

Figure 6.1. Some of the authors' favorite digital tools for assessing reading.

Evernote (www.evernote.com). Evernote is a tool that allows the user to create notebooks and then notes within a notebook. This tool can take the place of a binder or paper notebook for documenting student growth in reading. Evernote allows you to create student notebooks as well as class notebooks and easily share with other Evernote users. It provides flexibility by syncing all of your content, giving you access from anywhere you have an Internet connection. This means that you can quickly document student progress and work whether you're on a smartphone, tablet, or computer. Additionally, Evernote allows users to create text as well as insert images and audio to those texts. In Chapter 3, we reference this tool as an option that Franki's principal chose when she was looking for a way to take and store observation notes quickly and easily.

Google Docs (drive.google.com). Google Docs is part of the Google Drive online productivity suite and is offered free to individuals and schools. Drive is composed of five basic tools, all of which have possibilities for reading assessment because they can be accessed from any device with an Internet connection, they can be shared quickly and easily, and they all give teachers the ability to collaborate in real time.

- Docs—Word-processing tool (similar to Word) through which multiple teachers can record observations on an ongoing basis to show students' growth and achievement. Whether used to keep an ongoing conferring notebook or to share documents and observations with other teachers, Docs has become an integral piece of many classrooms.
- Slides—Presentation tool (similar to PowerPoint) with which students can add their own artifacts throughout the year and showcase their work for student-led conferences or a digital portfolio.
- Drawings—Illustration tool that allows students to visualize their thinking using a variety of shapes and text. This is a good tool for mind mapping and making connections between characters or concepts in a text.
- Sheets—Spreadsheet tool (similar to Excel) with which students and teachers can track progress, create graphs, and analyze data over time.
- Forms—Online survey tool that can be used to collect a variety of information from students. Students can log their daily or weekly reading, which the teacher can collect, analyze, and respond to. Student can also respond

continued on next page

Figure 6.1. Continued.

to reading and set goals on a form created by the teacher. Because Google Forms collects the information in a Google Sheet, teachers have the ability to see a whole class at one time or to see one student's growth over time.

Spring Reading Goals

* Required

Name *

[   ]

What is a book you've loved lately?

[   ]

What did you love about it?

[   ]

What are you most proud of as a reader in the last few months?

[   ]

What has been challenging for you as a reader lately?

[   ]

continued on next page

Figure 6.1. Continued.

Photos are invaluable artifacts of information for telling the story of a reader. They can be taken easily and without interruption on a smartphone or tablet during whole-class lessons, small-group instruction, or individual conferences. Once taken, they can be sent to Evernote and placed in the appropriate notebook or stored in Google Drive as an artifact of student work and progress. Photos of pages read, sticky notes used, written samples, and more can be recorded, archived, and referred to at any moment. If you are an Evernote user, the Evernote app has a camera feature that will place a photo directly into a notebook. Additionally, Google Plus (plus.google.com) lets you store and share photos online.

Student annotations have always been an important part of reading assessment. Being able to track the strategies a child uses gives us a great deal of information about the child's process. We may still collect sticky notes and reading notebooks, but many ebooks have annotation capabilities that allow the reader to highlight and take notes digitally. These digital annotations are often more flexible and provide a great deal of information on a child's reading life. Most ebook readers allow students to annotate a text they are reading, but some other tools can help with that as well. Diigo (www.diigo.com) lets students collaboratively annotate webpages for future reference, and mobile tools like Skitch (www.evernote.com/skitch) allow students to annotate images and screen captures.

Many tools help us to create **screen captures** on a computer or mobile device. Asking a child to think aloud while reading an online text allows us to see the decisions he or she is making along the way. Because online texts include hyperlinks, sidebars, tags, and more, screen capture tools can let us in on a child's process when reading a hyperlinked text. Free download tools like Jing (www.techsmith.com/jing) or online tools like Screencast-O-Matic (www.screencast-o-matic.com) let students create videos of their screen, talk through their thinking, and record that thinking as a way to reflect with their teacher. Additionally, mobile apps such as ScreenChomp (www.techsmith.com/screenchomp.html) and Explain Everything (found in the app store for your mobile device) allow students to illustrate their thinking and record themselves as they reflect.

Kidblog or other blogging tools provide students a space for ongoing writing about their learning. Often students use their blog space to write about or respond to the books they read. These posts are automatically archived and constitute a wonderful ongoing tool for assessment.

Video and audio files allow us to capture reading, conversations, book clubs, and more. Instead of merely taking notes on a conversation, we can watch the conversation for specific behaviors and strategies. These files are also great for self-assessment. Summarizing the information may still be important, but having a record of the entire conversation or reading often proves invaluable.

Digital Portfolios

Digital portfolios are another way to collect artifacts of our readers. While they are more complex and involved than some of the other assessment options, digital portfolios allow students to showcase their work both inside and outside the classroom. Each one of the assessment tools we have addressed can be held or linked to in these portfolios. In *Digital Student Portfolios: A Whole School Approach to Connected Learning and Continuous Assessment*, Matt Renwick claims that the most important role of a digital portfolio is "compiling a dynamic collection of information from many sources, in many forms and with many purposes, all aimed at presenting the most complete story possible of a student's learning experience" (14).

As we've mentioned in other chapters, one of the biggest impacts of the digital age is that the audience for a student's work can be exponentially larger than it once was. No longer does an assignment have to exist inside the four walls of the classroom. This audience now extends to parents, family, and friends and can serve the same purpose as a blog. Digital student portfolios have the potential to not only show understanding of each student's reading and comprehension, but also to illustrate a student's understanding of the technologies involved. Students can teach visitors about what they're learning and showcase their understanding in a variety of ways. The portfolio itself can be as simple as a PowerPoint or Google Slides presentation, with students continually adding their work and reflections to slides that they then share with their teacher. But it can also be as complex as an entire website or wiki on which students organize their work and highlight their progress over time. Tools such as Google Sites (sites.google.com), Weebly (www .weebly.com), and Wikispaces (www.wikispaces.com) offer students an online space to present their digital portfolios and store their work and thinking.

Student-Led Conferences

For the last few years, one of the middle schools that I (Bill) work with has been holding student-led conferences where, during the typical parent–teacher conference time, students describe what they have been working on, what they are proud of, and what their goals are. This practice has switched the conversation from grades and behavior to learning and achievement. Students generally create PowerPoint presentations and walk through some of the work done in class, but one teacher noticed that the conversations were too disconnected from one meeting to the next. She wanted to see the entire body of work that her sixth graders were creating over the course of the year, but instead each trimester constituted its own distinct set of units, and students looked only at the work for that set period of time. She wanted something more authentic, long-lasting—something that would incorporate digital tools beyond the PowerPoint presentations. Through many conversations, we developed a plan for using digital portfolios as a way to showcase student work and create the longevity she was looking for. At the time, we chose to use a simple wiki (www.pbwiki.com) as our platform and gave each student his or her own space to host the work. This collaborative online space allowed multiple students to work together and share their writing and class assignments with a broader audience in a way that couldn't be done with a file that is stored on an individual computer.

When conferences came around the following year, students were asked to speak about their work in broader terms, summarizing and explaining their progress throughout the year. Each conference session built on the one before, and students made connections between trimesters, showing how they had improved and setting goals for the next trimester. Talking to students about it later, I could see clearly that they were empowered. One student commented, "I like the portfolio. It lets me see where I've been and lets me know where I'm going. I feel like I'm more in control and I can add to it even at home. It's not a folder in my classroom that holds my stuff."

Sometimes it's difficult for students and parents to make the connection between a digital portfolio and reading because most of the work that is housed in this portfolio is work that a student has created. However, as we pointed out earlier in this book, the act of writing is inextricable from the act of reading and vice versa. Especially in the digital realm, what students read directly impacts the way they write and, in turn, what they write influences the way they read. In their portfolios, students can not only track their reading, but through their responses to that reading they will also be able to show how they've grown as readers and reflect on their reading lives.

Taking this classroom project one step further, other teachers have begun to combine the digital portfolios of the students in their class as a way to highlight work that illustrates the overall learning in the class as a whole. This type of portfolio becomes a showcase for the classroom community. Through this collaborative portfolio, students not only show their learning, but also help parents understand how digital tools are impacting education. Hearing about these educational practices from adults is one thing; learning about them from one's own child is another.

Bringing It All Together

Clearly, there are great differences in the options available between traditional and digital reading assessments. Just as in reading instruction, no one path or strategy will serve all students in all situations, so it's important to choose wisely based on your goals. For any one of the tools mentioned in this chapter there are ten more available that do something similar, and they are always evolving, adding new features and making it easier to manage the results users get. The tools of assessment have changed, and with all the options available, we suggest that you simply choose one or two that will meet your needs and go from there. Again, when using technology with students, it's easy to focus on assessing their use of technology rather than the goals you have set for learning. Each of the tools listed previously contains elements that you could assess in terms of how well your students can use the tools, and there is a place for that. But when it comes to assessing students' digital reading growth, always keep your eye on literacy and your goals. Use these tools for exactly what they are—tools that can make your grading practices more effective or more efficient—and spend your time focusing on what your students need to continue their reading journeys.

One final word about assessment: regardless of your assessment practices, it's important to keep parents and families in the loop. Many of your students and their families may never have heard of some of the tools we discuss in this chapter, so it is vital that any assessment you share with them is fully transparent. In the next chapter, we focus on how the tools you use in class can help to bring literacy practices and education into your students' homes. As you introduce new tools for assessment, it's always a good idea to continue communicating and letting everyone know how and why you're using these tools with their children.

Beyond the Classroom Walls: Connecting Digital Reading at Home and School

A few years ago, my (Franki's) students created a project in which they designed a dream playground. Using giant graph paper and paint, they worked collaboratively, learning about maps and geography, and ultimately constructed a map of their playgrounds. They were proud of their creations and, when the projects had been completed and shared, were excited to share them with their parents and families. Since these were group projects, however, not everyone could take them home. Groups made their own decisions about how to fairly decide who would take the project home. While some used a rock-paper-scissors strategy to determine the winner of the playground, others held discussions about who would use it most at home, while still other groups cut the project into several pieces, with each member taking a piece home. Regardless of the solution, not everyone was completely happy with the result.

I recall this scene as I reflect on our current relationships with students' families. We have slowly moved toward developing better ways to share work with families and to create a more equitable situation for all involved. Taking a project home is really a conversation starter for children, an answer to the question, "What did you do in school today?" As a parent who stores boxes of "projects" in our basement that my two daughters have brought home from school, I realize it was the conversations around these projects—not the projects themselves—that truly mattered most. For years these finished, tangible products and papers were the best ways teachers had to openly communicate with parents about what was going on in the classroom. Still, no matter how hard we've worked to open those lines of communication, the tools did not allow parents to see the vast amount of work that goes on in the course of a school day.

Thank goodness technology has opened up the ways in which we not only communicate with parents but actually make them a part of their child's learning experience. Digital tools have made the connection between school and home so much more effective because we are no longer confined to the space of the classroom or the time constraints of the school day. Parents can engage in their child's learning on a daily basis and in a variety of ways. Digital tools have also expanded the notion of communication so that we can now communicate our learning beyond our school community.

These digital forms of parent communication, whether a class website, a Twitter account, or some other tool, give parents ways to be more involved in their child's learning experience and also support students and parents as digital readers. By creating online places for families to learn about their child's learning, we are inviting families to be part of the digital reading community we've created in the classroom. When we use several forms of digital communication with our families, a number of benefits can be seen (see Figure 7.1). These benefits help us to continue building relationships between schools and the communities they serve. But building relationships through digital measures means we have to make sure parents understand the tools we're using at school. Parents today are in a tough spot because they are not always familiar with advances in technology and often see their kids as the "experts" when it comes to using these tools. They may even assume that, because their children were born in a digital era, the skills and strategies needed to survive today are already part of their genetic makeup. In many cases, parents are learning alongside their children, and for students to see technology as a tool for literacy, it is important to involve parents in that journey. Teachers need to offer opportunities for schools and families to connect around these topics and make meaning of them together.

Figure 7.1. Benefits of digital communication with families.

- **Students have more opportunities for learning at home.** Online communication is not solely for parents. With digital resources available at all times, students can access content, learn from peers, and begin conversations with parents about their learning. No longer is learning confined to the school day since much interaction can continue at home.
- **Parents have more access to the learning in the classroom.** Communication is no longer limited to a weekly newsletter, a final product, or a work sample. Instead, digital tools give parents an ongoing look into the classroom. They can see projects as they develop, and classroom videos offer parents the opportunity to listen in on classroom conversations. Twitter and Facebook updates give parents several ways to ask students about their school day that go well beyond, "What did you do in school today?"
- **Parents are invited to become digital readers.** Using digital tools to communicate with parents invites them on their child's digital reading journey. Regardless of their own experiences as digital readers, online spaces give parents ways to use the same kinds of tools their children are using in class, and parents in turn become models for digital reading as their children see them accessing school information.
- **Students become digital creators, which impacts digital reading.** Because most of the spaces teachers create require student input, students can learn the basics of digital communication. As a class of students tweets about the day, knowing their parents might be reading, they learn about choosing things worth sharing and being intentional in their word choice. When students work together to create a blog post, they are thinking about audience and purpose and taking those elements into account. These understandings will help them become more independent and critical readers of online content.
- **Parents receive some education on technology.** Parents of young children are often worried about the dangers of social networking sites and keeping kids safe online. Using many of the online tools available for communication allows parents to see these tools used in safe and effective ways. It also invites parents who are new to digital tools to begin exploring and invites families into a conversation about social networking. As families visit the class Facebook, Twitter, blog, or Instagram page together, they are learning about social networking and how to use these tools for learning. This can help relieve some of the fear associated with these online tools and open a dialogue between parents, student, and teacher around online safety.

Family Events

One of the ways we can extend learning beyond the school day that can have a dramatic impact on community outreach is through whole-school events that are put on by individual buildings or entire districts. This isn't a new concept. There have been plenty of opportunities in the past for parents and students to interact in the school environment. What may be different is the purpose behind them. Many of the programs traditionally held in schools are music concerts, art fairs, plays, and literacy nights, to name a few. These are great community-building activities that bring parents, students, and teachers together in a variety of ways. As education changes, however, we as educators must have a voice in explaining these changes. Whole-school programs can help us communicate these changes while giving community members opportunities to learn as well. This is a great way to educate parents on what it means to be literate in the digital age and what they should expect from their students in terms of reading digitally.

One common whole-school program that directly relates to the digital world—and is on most parents' minds—is an Internet safety night. It's no secret that many students are more adept at technology than their parents are, and the ability to navigate the Internet is just one example. So many parents fear what their children will be able to find on the Internet. While the Internet can bring an entire world of information to our fingertips, it also means that a number of things we may try to protect our kids from are no longer hidden. This dilemma presents challenges for parents and educators alike.

One year in one of my (Bill's) middle school buildings, we hosted an Internet safety night and invited the four feeder elementary schools. We wanted to conduct the event as a conversation to which students and parents could contribute, rather than as a presentation where they listen to someone talk for an hour. Enlisting the help of our local law enforcement, we began with a twenty-minute keynote during which Lieutenant Joseph Laramie, who is now director of the Missouri Internet Crimes Against Children Task Force (www.moicac.org), talked about the realities of the digital world and the need to teach kids how to be safe online. He discussed all the ways that technology is helping us as a society and how the Internet has ultimately changed much of the way we work and play. "But," he reminded us, "that doesn't mean there isn't a dark side. Education is our best defense against the predators and scams on the Internet. We can't ban our kids from being online. They're already there. What we can do is teach them how to be safe and responsible."

After his talk, Lieutenant Laramie was available for individual conversations, but attendees had other options as well. We made available computer labs for middle school families to get an introduction to Facebook, another room where a teacher talked about managing your digital footprint (how you are represented online) and what it means for students to publish work online, and a different session at which a teacher discussed the technology used in the classroom, providing examples and hands-on activities for families to explore some of the tools available to students. Twenty minutes later, families moved on to visit another room and engage in another discussion based on their student's grade level and interest. What we ultimately wanted from this event was to foster the beginning of a conversation both between school and families and between parents and students. After the event, my principal received many thanks from parents. This, they reported, was the opening they needed with their kids. They knew that being safe online is extremely important, but they didn't have the expertise to know where to start. This event gave them that entry point.

There are endless possibilities for whole-school programs focused on the same goals and parent involvement. Some schools choose to offer technology-based options during some of the events they are already holding at school. One elementary school hosted a technology open house on parent–teacher conference night where parents experienced digital tools as their kids would. When my district installed SMART Boards in classrooms, for example, parents were invited into some of our schools to learn about them and see how teachers and students were going to use them. In many cases, the students themselves led their parents through some exercises and gave them the opportunity to interact with the board. When we implemented BYOD, teachers, students, and parents all had some learning to do around how to use the tools for educational purposes. "How will we manage learning if everyone has different devices?" was the question asked by parents and teachers again and again. So we offered a technology petting zoo where librarians and teachers introduced tools such as Google Docs, Evernote, and Padlet that can be used on any device with an Internet connection. For these sessions, parents were encouraged to bring in their own devices or to use the laptops, Google Chromebooks, and tablets that students had access to during the school day. By reaching out to parents and familiarizing them with the tools their students will use every day, schools can reinforce that technology and the Internet are more than just Angry Birds and other online games. They provide an educational context for the devices, and, if done skillfully, teachers can also highlight some of the digital reading skills and tools they're working on with their students.

A Word of Warning

Even with the best intentions, schools must be very careful about the messages they give to parents. Not long ago, I (Bill) sat in on a presentation for parents of elementary kids titled "Literacy in the 21st Century." The topics were what you might expect a typical literacy presentation to include: the importance of reading at home on a regular basis and how parents can work at home to support the reading skills and practices their children are doing at school. What was disappointing was the cursory mention of the role technology plays in reading in this "21st century" presentation. The speakers were all well intentioned, but the message was that "technology plays a role in what it means to be literate now" with a list of external websites, displayed on the projector, where parents could go to get more information about literacy. Upon going to all of the websites listed, I found no mention of digital texts. Instead, they were all tools and strategies for helping kids to read traditional texts. As I talked to some of the parents who were in attendance, it was clear that the message (perhaps unintended) was that technology is still separate from reading. The message they received in the session was that the Internet is simply a place to find more information on literacy instruction rather than its own space where reading happens.

We relay this story simply to say that, while these teachers had great intentions and are good teachers, the planning for such an event is crucial in order to deliver the right message. As educators it's easy to get caught up in what's going on in our classrooms and schools and forget that, when parents come to an event, we get only a limited time with them. There's always so much information to share that we focus on getting through everything rather than on our message about technology and literacy. The question that must always be asked is, "What do we want them to know, understand, or think about when they leave?" It's not enough simply to provide resources for parents and let them explore on their own. Parents are busy, just as we are, and if we leave their learning up to chance, it won't happen. We have to be intentional and make our time together meaningful. See Figure 7.2 for some preliminary questions to ask yourself before meeting with students' families.

Setting Up for Communication That Makes a Difference

The principles and considerations behind the whole school events just described could easily transfer to an individual teacher's outreach to the parents of the students in his or her classroom. Working with parents in this smaller setting lets you also take a more individualized approach to the needs of your students and the ways in which you integrate technology. A good first step is to design a classroom communication plan that harnesses the power of digital tools to reach outside the classroom. For this digital communication to meet all of the needs we hope it will meet, teachers must plan the components they will share with parents in an intentional way. Just as we are intentional about the tools we use with our students, we must be intentional about the tools we use to extend the school day beyond the classroom walls.

We have lots of options when designing communication for the school year. We want enough of a variety to meet the needs of all families, but we also want to be able to manage the tools we use. Thinking about our goals helps us to do this more efficiently. One year, I (Franki) was setting up online tools for home

Figure 7.2. Considerations for parent outreach events on digital literacy.

1. *What is our focus?* During the time we have, we can't cover everything that's important; if we attempt to do so, we muddy the message. What's vital for families to know and what is our purpose for the event?

2. *Who is the audience?* While this may seem obvious, we try to think about the specific parents or community members who are coming. What groundwork has already been laid with them? Is this the beginning of the conversation or have there already been other sessions? The audience may change and may be mixed in terms of experience with the topic, but it's important to not be too repetitive so that there's something new for everyone.

3. *How will this event support students as digital readers?* Schools hold many types of events throughout the school year, so it's important to think about where digital reading fits and how the event will support students as digital readers.

4. *What resources do we want to provide to our community?* Can we create a page on our school website that is updated regularly where we can highlight websites, apps, and programs that we believe will support digital reading strategies and provide digital content for student and family use?

5. *Is this event for families or is it specifically for parents or caregivers?* Based on the goals of an event, who should attend? If this is a family event, as you plan be sure to recognize that, just like your students, family members will have a wide variety of experiences around digital reading. Try to create multiple opportunities and entry points so that everyone in attendance will have a place to start.

6. *How does this topic relate to them as parents and to their kids?* When community members come to the school, are they coming to be informed about a topic (e.g., Internet safety), or is it more about the experience they will have (e.g., technology open house)? How is this directly applicable at home? For these kinds of events, simply informing them of what you're doing at school isn't enough. What can they do with the information you're presenting to them?

7. *What is your call to action?* When community members leave your event, what do you want them to do? It's important to be very specific about what the call to action is. Obviously, you can't make them do anything, and you're merely suggesting some strategies or things to try, but for those who have taken the time to come to your event, there's a good chance they will also make the effort to take action after the fact.

and school communication. In doing so, I set the following goals for the year. My students and I wanted to:

- have a variety of audiences and formats to choose from when sharing;
- connect with classmates, families, and more global audiences;
- have space to share a variety of learning that includes blog posts, videos, photos, classroom activities, and general information;

- share with a purpose instead of sharing to meet the requirements of an assignment;
- share individual work and information with individual parents;
- have a variety of ways to gather information or ask for input from families and others;
- reflect on learning over time;
- understand the power of connecting with families and beyond; and
- learn safety associated with online sharing.

Because there are so many options for connecting and communicating beyond the classroom, forming my goals first was key. If my goal had just been "communication and information sharing," a basic website would suffice. But if I wanted the communication to truly impact families *and* my students, it was important that my students be involved in creating these communications so the connection would be seamless. As they thought about audience and purpose, students would more easily know where to direct families for information and communication and how to better understand these same types of communication shared by others.

To meet the listed goals, I created the plan outlined in Figure 7.3 for the coming school year. Connecting home and school by giving parents and families opportunities to be digital readers together is a big goal of these communications, helps to bridge the home–school gap for students, and can potentially give everyone involved more digital reading experience.

Figure 7.3. School year plan for introducing families to digital communications.

Classroom Website and Blog. The class website serves as the hub of communication and houses basic information as well as links to other classroom communication avenues (listed below). Here students can find the online sources for digital reading, book trailers, and classroom announcements that they will use in class, giving them easy and consistent access. Because the site allows for a variety of media types (text, hyperlinks, videos, presentations, etc.), students can easily extend learning from our classroom to their homes and stay connected to the classroom and their reading.

Kidblog. Each child has an individual Kidblog (www.kidblog.org) account that is connected only to our classroom, giving students a place to share things about their learning they are interested in sharing only with a close group (classmates and families). Parents are given their child's password so they can be active participants in the community by commenting and using the space to learn about the classroom. Here students will reflect on their reading and have a safe, controlled environment in which to comment and begin to understand how to read and write in an online space.

continued on next page

Figure 7.3. Continued.

Facebook and Twitter Accounts. Facebook (www.facebook.com) and Twitter (www.twitter .com) are two of the most widely used social networks currently online. In our classroom, we use these social accounts throughout the day in shared settings to communicate our learning, share what we're reading and the online resources we've found or used that day, and make class announcements, all of which gives parents a glimpse of our school day. We decide at class meetings what to share in these two accounts, as well as which other teachers and classrooms to connect with so we can see the kinds of things other classrooms share and learn from them. By having both types of accounts, we can reach more families, as some may be active on one network but not the other. And, because we can make each of these accounts private, we can experiment in the safety of our classroom.

Google Calendar. Replacing the traditional classroom "planner" with an embedded Google Calendar (calendar.google.com) helps students and families get into the habit of checking our class website and keeping tabs on what we're doing in class. Through this tool, families can access the online calendar for announcements, homework, and special events and stay up-to-date. Families who already use Google Calendar personally can even add the classroom calendar to their personal calendar and be immediately updated on events.

Google Docs and Google Forms. Our district, like many, is a Google Apps for Education district (https://www.google.com/work/apps/education), and Google provides a natural way for students to access learning from anywhere. Having access to their Google documents that are in progress or to documents that others have shared with them allows students to share learning with their families at home before something is "finished." Google also lets us collect and share information quickly and easily through the use of Forms, an online survey tool. Because students can access this from anywhere, they can read data that they collect, review the work of a classmate, or share their reading with other students. In Chapter 6, we reference Google Docs and Forms as a way for teachers to collect and maintain assessment data.

Digital Bulletin Boards. Students often share their work during reading workshop share sessions, or they share insights from a book talk with the class. Other times we create charts about how a character in our read-alouds is changing over time. These learning experiences have been hard to capture, but digital tools have made it easier and let us archive our in-class conversations for future use. Giving parents access to digital bulletin boards we've shared as a class and also creating digital versions of classroom charts are ways to connect home and school and allow the conversation to continue after the school day. These boards also connect learning through a video of the actual conversation in which learning occurred.

Class Pinterest Board. A Pinterest (www.pinterest.com) board allows us to share our learning in a visual way. Visual sharing is critical for familiarizing students with a variety of ways to read and share information. These boards showcase visuals of learning happening in our classroom and connect parents to our work. Often we share what we're reading as well as strategies and other resources that parents can use to have conversations with students about what they are reading in class.

There is no magic to the combination of tools that will allow you to extend learning beyond the school walls; however, the combination described here meets the needs and goals I have for my students at this time. Knowing that all of them may not "take off" and that I may need to add something that seems missing later in the school year, I can be flexible and use what works for both my students and their families. The key is having a plan with goals for communication that supports literacy in multiple ways and involves families as digital readers.

Postscript

Our collaboration began in 2008 when we both served on the Executive Committee of NCTE. As part of our work that year, we helped write the definition of *21st century literacies* as well as the *NCTE Framework for 21st Century Curriculum and Assessment* (http://www.ncte.org/governance/21stcenturyframework). That experience allowed us to closely study issues and ideas that were becoming critical to literacy teachers. We became passionate about the need to embed technology in the classroom in a way that stays true to the beliefs about literacy and learning we've always held.

For the purposes of this book, which is part of the Principles in Practice strand titled Reading in Today's Classrooms, based on NCTE's *Reading Instruction for All Students* policy research brief, we have had to separate reading out of the whole of literacy. Doing so invited us to be thoughtful about classroom practice in new ways. But we know that reading cannot be viewed in isolation or apart from writing, listening, and speaking. We know that *literacy* is a word that encompasses all of these.

Throughout the writing of the book, we knew that our bigger goals as literacy teachers were part of the *NCTE Framework for 21st Century Curriculum and Assessment* that NCTE had already established. This book came about because of our understanding of the framework. Without that, digital reading would be something far less meaningful.

We believe the framework gives the book a larger context and reminds us, as educators, that we are going for something more holistic than skilled readers. We want our students to be active communicators in the complex world they live in. The definition, the framework, and the embedded questions have been the basis of all of our work since they were written. As you move forward in your journey as a literacy teacher in the digital age, we hope you find these as useful as we have.

Annotated Bibliography

Harvey, Stephanie, Anne Goudvis, Katherine
Muhtaris, and Kristin Ziemke
**Connecting Comprehension and Technology:
Adapt and Extend Toolkit Practices**
Portsmouth: Firsthand, 2013. Print.

Harvey and Goudvis have teamed up with two
classroom teachers to create a book that shows
what is possible when digital tools are embedded
in the comprehension work already being done in
the classroom. The focus of the book is on tools
for thinking, and it is filled with classroom examples that demonstrate how digital tools expand
what is possible for our young readers. For those
who know the work of Harvey and Goudvis, this
will be a welcome additional resource for teachers on how to extend the ideas of their earlier
comprehension work to include digital tools. For
teachers looking for ideas on ways to begin using
digital tools with elementary children, this book is
filled with stories and examples.

Hicks, Troy
The Digital Writing Workshop
Portsmouth: Heinemann, 2009. Print.

In this groundbreaking book, Hicks asks us to
think about the ways in which digital tools must
change how we live in the classroom each day. An
expert in writing workshop and a director of the
National Writing Project, Hicks explores the ways
that digital tools can make writing more relevant
and authentic. He explores each component of
the writing workshop and gives readers a great
deal to think about as we become comfortable
with this expanded definition of what it means to
be a writer. He reminds us that writing can't be
about assignments and that digital writing must
be grounded in what we know as writing teachers
first.

Kajder, Sara
**Adolescents and Digital Literacies: Learning
Alongside Our Students**
Urbana: NCTE, 2010. Print.

Using interviews and other classroom examples,
Kadjer focuses not on the technology that has
such an impact on the lives of students and
teachers but instead on how that technology has
changed teaching practices. She makes the case
for embracing the reading and writing experiences
that students already have in their daily lives and
asks us to bring those authentic, real-life experiences into our lessons and meld the in-school and
out-of-school literacies into an inclusive literacy
that everyone can value.

McLeod, Scott, and Chris Lehmann, eds.
**What School Leaders Need to Know about
Digital Technologies and Social Media.**
San Francisco: Jossey-Bass, 2012. Print.

This book is a compilation of pieces written by
leaders in educational technology exploring the
ways that technology and social media are impacting schools and educators around the world. Each
chapter is dedicated to a different technology with
classroom examples and suggestions while at the
same time making the case that building and district leaders must use these tools to better connect
with the students and families they serve. School
leaders get an overview of each of these technologies along with practical examples that can be
implemented immediately.

Renwick, Matt
**Digital Student Portfolios: A Whole School
Approach to Connected Learning and
Continuous Assessment**
Virginia Beach: Powerful Learning Practice,
2014. Ebook.

Matt Renwick, an elementary principal in Wisconsin, shares the journey his school has taken to implement digital portfolios, sharing the ways in which these portfolios combine formative and summative assessment. But the true power of digital portfolios comes from the ownership children have taken for their own learning. Not only does Renwick discuss issues around assessment, but also the ebook format allows us to examine digital projects students have completed. The ways in which technology is authentically embedded into students' learning is persuasive; teachers can learn a great deal from Renwick about digital literacy in an elementary school.

Richardson, Will
Blogs, Wikis, Podcasts and Other Powerful Web Tools for Classrooms
Thousand Oaks: Corwin, 2010. Print.

Richardson's book is one we revisit often as we move forward in our understanding of digital literacy. He offers a close look at a variety of Web tools that can be used in the classroom, shares his understanding of each tool, and provides suggestions for using those tools with students. The book combines Richardson's knowledge of online tools with his understanding of literacy to create a resource that can help teachers implement these tools in authentic ways.

Richardson, Will, and Mancabelli, Rob
Personal Learning Networks: Using the Power of Connections to Transform Education
Bloomington: Solution Tree, 2011. Print.

Richardson and Mancabelli highlight the power of teachers using technology and the Internet to quickly and easily connect with one another in order to share ideas and create a network around educational practices. They remind us that we are more powerful together and that we can truly enact changes in education that will benefit our students. By focusing on the ever important connections between people, the authors encourage us to look outside our physical classrooms and buildings.

Sheninger, Eric
Digital Leadership: Changing Paradigms for Changing Times
Thousand Oaks: Corwin, 2014. Print.

Telling your school's story is the focus of this book. Eric Sheninger is a high school principal committed to using digital tools to empower students and teachers. This book looks at the impact of digital tools on the classroom as well as on the entire school community. It reminds us how critical it is for schools to have a leader who is committed to moving forward and embracing all that is possible for our students.

Works Cited

Applegate, Katherine. *The One and Only Ivan*. New York: Harper. 2012. Print.

Anthony, Jessica, and Rodrigo Corral. *Chopsticks*. New York: Razorbill, 2012. Print.

Atwell, Nancie. *In the Middle: New Understandings about Writing, Reading, and Learning*. 2nd ed. Portsmouth: Boynton/Cook-Heinemann, 1998. Print.

Aungst, G., & Zucker, L. *All About Explorers: Christopher Columbus*. AllAboutExplorers.com. 2006. Web. 10 Sept. 2013.

Ayres, Ruth, and Christi Overman. *Celebrating Writers: From Possibilities through Publication*. Portland: Stenhouse, 2013. Print.

Basij-Rasikh, Shabana. "Dare to Educate Afghan Girls." Video. *Ted*.com. TED, Dec. 2012. Web. 25 Nov. 2014.

Beers, Kylene, and Robert E. Probst. *Notice and Note: Strategies for Close Reading*. Portsmouth: Heinemann, 2013. Print.

Bellairs, John. *The Trolley to Yesterday*. New York: Puffin, 1989. Print.

Berger, Ron. *Austin's Butterfly*. Vimeo. 2014. Video. 8 Jan. 2015.

Calkins, Lucy McCormick. *The Art of Teaching Reading*. New York: Pearson, 2001. Print.

———. "Get Real about Reading." *Instructor* 106.8 (1997): n. pag. *Scholastic*. Web. 1 Jan. 2015.

Clive, Sophie Windsor, and Liberty Smith. *Murmuration*. YouTube. 2 Dec. 2011. Web. 8 Jan. 2015.

Cole, Louis. *Hope in the Dust*. FunforLouis [Vlog]. YouTube. Feb. 2014. Web. 8 Jan. 2015.

Crump, Marty. *The Mystery of Darwin's Frog*. Honesdale: Boyds Mills, 2013. Print.

Dalton, Bridget, and C. Patrick Proctor. "The Changing Landscape of Text and Comprehension in the Age of New Literacies." *Handbook of Research on New Literacies*. Ed. Julie Coiro, Michele Knobel, Colin Lankshear, and Donald J. Leu. Mahwah: Erlbaum, 2008. 297–324. Print.

DiTerlizzi, Tony. *The Search for WondLa*. New York: Simon, 2012. Print.

"For Good." Kristin Chenoweth, Sarah Good, and the Los Angeles Philharmonic at the Hollywood Bowl. YouTube. 24 Aug. 2013. Video. 8 Jan. 2015.

Fried, Robert L. *The Game of School: Why We All Play It, How It Hurts Kids, and What It Will Take to Change It*. San Francisco: Jossey-Bass, 2005. Print.

Graff, Lisa. *The Thing about Georgie*. New York: HarperTrophy, 2008. Print.

Grimes, Nikki. *Hopscotch Love: A Family Treasury of Love Poems*. New York: Lothrop, Lee & Shepard. 1999. Print.

Guiberson, Brenda Z. *Frog Song*. New York: Holt, 2013. Print.

Hatkoff, Juliana, Isabella Hatkoff, and Craig Hatkoff. *Winter's Tail: How One Little Dolphin Learned to Swim Again*. New York: Scholastic, 2009. Print.

Harvey, Stephanie, and Anne Goudvis. *Strategies That Work: Teaching Comprehension to Enhance Understanding*. Portland: Stenhouse, 2000. Print.

Harvey, Stephanie, Anne Goudvis, Katherine Muhtaris, and Kristin Ziemke. *Connecting Comprehension and Technology: Adapt and Extend Toolkit Practices*. Portsmouth: Firsthand, 2013. Print.

Hicks, Troy. *The Digital Writing Workshop*. Portsmouth: Heinemann, 2009. Print.

Hopkins, Lee Bennett. *Lives: Poems about Famous Americans*. New York: HarperCollins. 1999. Print.

Javernick, Ellen, and Colleen M. Madden. *What If Everybody Did That?* Tarrytown: Cavendish, 2010. Print.

Johnston, Peter H. *Choice Words: How Our Language Affects Children's Learning*. Portland: Stenhouse, 2004. Print.

Joyce, William, and Joe Bluhm. *The Fantastic Flying Books of Mr. Morris Lessmore*. New York: Atheneum, 2012. Print.

Keene, Ellin Oliver, and Susan Zimmermann. *Mosaic of Thought: The Power of Comprehension Strategy Instruction*. 2nd ed. Portsmouth: Heinemann, 2007. Print.

Kittle, Penny. *Book Love: Developing Depth, Stamina, and Passion in Adolescent Readers*. Portsmouth: Heinemann, 2013. Print.

———. "Elements of a Reading Workshop to Increase Stamina, Fluency, and Joy." *Penny Kittle*. Penny Kittle, n.d. Web. 16 Jan. 2014.

Landrigan, Clare, and Tammy Mulligan. *Assessment in Perspective: Focusing on the Readers Behind the Numbers*. Portland: Stenhouse, 2013. Print.

Laramie, Joseph. "Staying Safe Online." Missouri Internet Crimes Against Children Task Force, 2010. Presentation.

Lloyd, Natalie. *A Snicker of Magic*. New York: Scholastic, 2014. Print.

Maiers, Angela. "Tech Comfy NOT Tech Savvy!" *AngelaMaiers*. Angela Maiers, 10 Aug. 2010. Web. 15 Aug. 2010.

Mermelstein, Leah. *Don't Forget to Share: The Crucial Last Step in the Writing Workshop*. Portsmouth: Heinemann, 2007. Print.

Morrison, Gretchen. Personal interview. 16 Oct. 2013.

Mulligan, Andy. *Trash*. New York: Ember, 2010. Print.

Myers, Walter Dean. *Lockdown*. New York: HarperTeen/Amistad. 2010. Print.

National Council of Teachers of English. *Formative Assessment That* Truly *Informs Instruction*. Urbana: NCTE, 2013. Print.

———. *The NCTE Definition of 21st Century Literacies*. Urbana: NCTE, 2013. Print.

———. *NCTE Framework for 21st Century Curriculum and Assessment*. Urbana: NCTE, 2013. Print.

———. *Reading Instruction for* All *Students: A Policy Research Brief*. Urbana: NCTE, 2012. Print.

National Geographic. *World's Weirdest: Frog Father "Spits Out" Young*. National Geographic WILD. n.d. Web. 8 Jan. 2015.

National Governors Association Center for Best Practices, and Council of Chief State School Officers. *Common Core State Standards for English Language Arts and Literacy in History/Social Studies, Science, and Technical Subjects*. Washington, DC: 2010. Print.

Nielsen, Jennifer A. *The False Prince*. New York: Scholastic. 2012. Print.

O'Connor, Barbara. *How to Steal a Dog*. New York: Square Fish, 2007. Print.

Palacio, R. J. *Wonder*. New York: Random, 2012. Print.

Pearson, Ridley. *The Kingdom Keepers: Disney after Dark*. New York: Disney, 2005. Print.

Renwick, Matt. *Digital Student Portfolios: A Whole School Approach to Connected Learning and Continuous Assessment*. Virginia Beach: Powerful Learning Practice, 2014. E-book.

Reynolds, Peter H. *The Dot*. Cambridge: Candlewick, 2003. Print.

Ripp, Pernille. *My Students' Classroom Vision*. Blogging through the Fourth Dimension [Blog]. 9 Sept. 2013. Web. 8 Jan. 2015.

Rosenblatt, Louise M. *Literature as Exploration*. New York: Appleton-Century, 1938. Print.

Sibberson, Franki, and Karen Szymusiak. *Still Learning to Read: Teaching Students in Grades 3–6*. Portland: Stenhouse, 2003. Print.

Soderberg, Erin. *The Quirks: Welcome to Normal*. New York: Bloomsbury, 2013. Print.

Stepp, Laura Sessions. *Our Last Best Shot: Guiding Our Children through Early Adolescence*. New York: Riverhead, 2000. Print.

Taberski, Sharon. *On Solid Ground: Strategies for Teaching Reading K–3*. Portsmouth: Heinemann, 2000. Print.

"Tree." TOI Lead India Advertisement. YouTube. 10 July 2008. Web. 8 Jan. 2015.

Wilbur, Matika. "Surviving Disappearance, Re-Imagining and Humanizing Native Peoples." Video. *Tedxtalks.ted.com*. TEDx Talks, 23 July 2013. Web. 25 Nov. 2014.

Willems, Mo. *Should I Share My Ice Cream?* New York: Hyperion, 2011. Print.

Yahgulanaas, Michael Nicoll, and Wangari Maathai. *The Little Hummingbird*. Vancouver: Greystone, 2010. Print.

Index

Authors

William L. Bass II is currently an innovation coordinator for instructional technology and library media in St. Louis, Missouri, and an adjunct professor of educational technology for Missouri Baptist University. As a former middle and high school English teacher, he focuses on systemic and sustainable integration of technology into classrooms at all grade levels. Bass is a Google Certified Teacher, a Google Education Trainer, and coauthor of the book *From Inspiration to Red Carpet: Host Your Own Student Film Festival* (2013). He blogs at Mr. Bass Online (mrbassonline.com) and is a Choice Literacy contributor (choiceliteracy.com). You can find him on Twitter as @billbass.

Franki Sibberson is currently a third-grade teacher in Dublin, Ohio, where she has been teaching for more than twenty-five years. Franki is the coauthor with Karen Szymusiak of many books and videos on teaching reading in the intermediate grades, including *Beyond Leveled Books: Supporting Early and Transitional Readers in Grades K–8* (2001), *Still Learning to Read: Teaching Students in Grades 3–6* (2003), and *Day-to-Day Assessment in the Reading Workshop: Making Informed Instructional Decisions in Grades 3–6* (2008). She is also the author of *The Joy of Planning: Designing Minilesson Cycles in Grades 3–6* (2012). Sibberson blogs with Mary Lee Hahn at A Year of Reading (readingyear.blogspot.com) and is a regular contributor to Choice Literacy (choiceliteracy.com). You can find her on Twitter as @frankisibberson.

Contributors

Cryslynn Billingsley teaches students in St. Louis, Missouri, and is a certified cognitive coach and administrator. After finishing her Educational Specialist certificate, she will pursue a doctorate in teaching and learning processes. Cryslynn can be found as @Ccblivelife on Twitter.

Maria Caplin is a fifth-grade teacher in Dublin, Ohio. She is also a Wonder Lead Ambassador for the National Center for Families Learning (NCFL). Caplin blogs at Teaching in the 21st Century (http://teachingin21.blogspot.com). She can be found as @mariacaplin on Twitter.

Ann Marie Corgill is a fourth-grade teacher at Cherokee Bend Elementary and has taught and learned in classrooms from first to sixth grade since 1994 in both Birmingham, Alabama, and New York City. She was named Alabama's 2014–2015 Teacher of the Year and is the author of *Of Primary Importance: What's Essential in Teaching Young Writers* (2008). Corgill is a teacher contributor for Choice Literacy, and you can find her at amclearningjourney.blogspot.com and @acorgill on Twitter.

Bev Gallagher is a third-grade teacher and director of educational outreach at Princeton Day School. She is passionate about literacy and eager to find new ways to integrate technology into reading and writing workshop. She blogs at http://whatmattersmostinteaching.blogspot.com and can be found as @3GallagherPDS on Twitter.

Katharine Hale teaches fifth grade at Abingdon Elementary, a Title I school in Arlington, Virginia. Hers is a one-to-one iPad classroom where students learn through reading and writing workshop, "flipped" lessons, social networking, and authentic experiences. She has had the honor of sharing her work on integrating technology in both math and literacy at conferences such as Literacy for All, ISTE, NCTE, and Arlington Public School's Festival of the Mind. She has also written a few articles for Choice Literacy. Hale's blog is teachitivity.wordpress.com, and you can follow her on Twitter as @mshale5thgrade.

Jillian Heise, a National Board Certified Teacher, has been teaching language arts and reading to seventh and eighth graders in the suburban Milwaukee area for ten years. She currently works with both grade levels at the Indian Community School of Milwaukee. Heise talks books and teaching on Twitter as @heisereads; her book blog is Heise Reads & Recommends (www.heisereads.com); and her teaching blog is Heise Teaches & Writes (heisewrites.blogspot.com).

Julie Johnson has taught for twenty-four years and currently teaches in Hilliard, Ohio. She is the 2010 recipient of the NCTE Donald H. Graves Writing Award. She blogs at raisingreadersandwriters.com and can be found on Twitter as @jreaderwriter.

Scott Jones is a fifth-grade teacher in Hilliard, Ohio, and has been designated Ohio Master Teacher. Follow him on Twitter as @escott818 or visit his class website, theflockjwr.com.

Tony Keefer is inspired daily by his fourth-grade language arts students in Dublin, Ohio. He passionately reads, writes, and watches soccer. You can find him on Twitter (@TonyKeefer) and his blogs (http://tonykeefer.blogspot.com/ and http://tonykeefer.tumblr.com/).

Katherine Sokolowski has taught for more than fifteen years in elementary schools and currently teaches fifth grade in the same small town in central Illinois where she grew up. She regularly writes about teaching on the website Choice Literacy and at her blog Read, Write, Reflect (http://readwriteandreflect.blogspot.com). You can find her on Twitter with the username @katsok.

Gretchen Taylor is a literacy coach for Dublin City Schools in Dublin, Ohio, and she is also a contributor to Choice Literacy. Previously, she spent nine years teaching sixth- and seventh-grade language arts at Sells Middle School in Dublin, Ohio.

Karen Terlecky has worked as a classroom teacher for more than thirty-three years and is currently a literacy coach for the Dublin [Ohio] City Schools. She has a passion for learning and motivating students to become lifelong readers and writers. In addition to her professional duties, she is a contributor to Choice Literacy. She can be found as @karenterlecky on Twitter and also blogs at Literate Lives (http://literatelives.blogspot.com).

This book was typeset in Janson Text and BotonBQ by
Barbara Frazier.

Typefaces used on the cover include American Typewriter,
Frutiger Bold, Formata Light, and Formata Bold.

The book was printed on 60-lb. White Recycled Offset paper
by Versa Press, Inc.

30% Total Recycled Fiber